Navigating Neurodiversity: A Guide for Parents of Neurodivergent Children

Table Of Contents

Chapter 1: Understanding Neurodiversity — 5

    Defining Neurodiversity — 5

    Recognizing the Strengths of Neurodivergent Children — 6

    Challenging Stereotypes and Misconceptions — 9

Chapter 2: Autism Spectrum Disorder (ASD) Support for Neurodivergent Children — 11

    Understanding Autism Spectrum Disorder — 11

    Early Signs and Diagnosis — 12

    Creating an Autism-Friendly Environment — 14

    Effective Communication Strategies — 16

    Developing Social Skills in Children with ASD — 18

Chapter 3: Attention Deficit Hyperactivity Disorder (ADHD) Resources for Neurodivergent Children — 20

    Understanding ADHD — 20

    Identifying ADHD Symptoms in Children — 22

    Managing ADHD Behaviors at Home and School — 23

    Developing Organization and Time Management Skills — 25

    Supporting Academic Success for Children with ADHD — 27

Navigating Neurodiversity: A Guide for Parents of Neurodivergent Children

Chapter 4: Sensory Processing Disorder Interventions for Neurodivergent Children   29

   Understanding Sensory Processing Disorder   29

   Recognizing Sensory Overload and Sensory Seeking Behaviors   31

   Creating a Sensory-Friendly Environment   32

   Sensory Integration Techniques and Therapies   34

Chapter 5: Learning Disabilities Assistance for Neurodivergent Children   36

   Understanding Learning Disabilities   36

   Identifying Different Types of Learning Disabilities   38

   Individualized Education Plans (IEPs) and 504 Plans   39

   Effective Teaching Strategies for Children with Learning Disabilities   41

   Supporting Homework and Study Skills   43

Chapter 6: Executive Functioning Skills Development for Neurodivergent Children   45

   Understanding Executive Functioning Challenges   45

   Improving Time Management and Organization Skills   46

   Enhancing Planning and Problem-Solving Abilities   48

   Developing Self-Monitoring and Self-Regulation Skills   50

Navigating Neurodiversity: A Guide for Parents of Neurodivergent Children

Chapter 7: Social Skills Training for Neurodivergent Children	52
Understanding the Importance of Social Skills	52
Teaching Social Skills at Home and School	54
Building Friendships and Peer Relationships	56
Navigating Social Challenges and Bullying	58
Chapter 8: Emotional Regulation Strategies for Neurodivergent Children	60
Understanding Emotional Regulation Difficulties	60
Teaching Emotional Awareness and Expression	62
Coping Strategies for Managing Strong Emotions	64
Promoting Emotional Resilience and Well-being	66
Chapter 9: Speech and Language Therapy for Neurodivergent Children	68
Understanding Speech and Language Disorders	68
Early Intervention and Assessment	70
Speech Therapy Techniques and Exercises	72
Supporting Language Development and Communication Skills	73
Chapter 10: Occupational Therapy for Neurodivergent Children	75

Understanding Occupational Therapy and its Benefits	75
Assessing Sensory Integration and Motor Skills	77
Occupational Therapy Interventions and Activities	79
Supporting Daily Living Skills and Independence	82
Chapter 11: Parenting Strategies for Raising Neurodivergent Children	84
Embracing a Strengths-Based Approach	84
Building a Supportive Network of Professionals and Peers	86
Practicing Self-Care and Stress Management	88
Advocating for Your Child's Needs	90
Nurturing Resilience and Confidence in Neurodivergent Children	92

Chapter 1: Understanding Neurodiversity

Defining Neurodiversity

In this subchapter, we will delve into the concept of neurodiversity and its significance in understanding and supporting neurodivergent children. Neurodiversity is a term that recognizes and celebrates the natural variations in neurological functioning and behavior. It emphasizes that neurological differences, such as Autism Spectrum Disorder (ASD), Attention Deficit Hyperactivity Disorder (ADHD), sensory processing disorder, learning disabilities, and executive functioning challenges, are simply part of the human diversity.

For parents of neurodivergent children, understanding neurodiversity is crucial as it helps reframe their perspective on their child's differences. Instead of viewing their child's neurodivergence as a deficiency or a problem to be fixed, they can embrace it as a unique way of being in the world.

Neurodiversity acknowledges that neurodivergent children have their own strengths and abilities, which may be different from the neurotypical population. By recognizing and nurturing these strengths, parents can help their children thrive.

This subchapter will explore various neurodivergent conditions and offer resources and interventions specific to each. For example, we will provide information on ASD support, including therapies, educational resources, and strategies for enhancing social skills and emotional regulation in autistic children. Similarly, we will discuss ADHD and provide resources for managing attention and impulsivity challenges, as well as techniques for improving executive functioning skills.

Navigating Neurodiversity: A Guide for Parents of Neurodivergent Children

We will also cover sensory processing disorder, learning disabilities, and speech and language therapy, offering practical interventions and tips for parents to support their child's needs in these areas. Additionally, we will explore occupational therapy and its benefits for neurodivergent children, focusing on sensory integration techniques and adaptive strategies for daily living.

Moreover, this subchapter will address the emotional and social aspects of raising neurodivergent children. We will provide parenting strategies that promote a positive and inclusive environment at home, fostering self-esteem and resilience in children.

By the end of this subchapter, parents will have a comprehensive understanding of neurodiversity and its implications for their child's development. They will be equipped with a range of resources and interventions tailored to their child's specific needs, enabling them to navigate the challenges and celebrate the strengths of their neurodivergent child.

Recognizing the Strengths of Neurodivergent Children

Neurodiversity is a concept that celebrates the unique neurological differences among individuals, including those with conditions such as Autism Spectrum Disorder (ASD), Attention Deficit Hyperactivity Disorder (ADHD), sensory processing disorder, learning disabilities, and more. As parents of neurodivergent children, it is crucial to recognize and embrace their strengths, as this can greatly enhance their overall wellbeing and development.

Navigating Neurodiversity: A Guide for Parents of Neurodivergent Children

One of the most important aspects of recognizing the strengths of neurodivergent children is understanding that their brains are wired differently. This means that they may excel in certain areas that neurotypical children may struggle with. For example, they may possess exceptional attention to detail, heightened creativity, or exceptional problem-solving skills. By identifying and nurturing these strengths, parents can help their children build self-confidence and achieve success in various aspects of their lives.

Autism Spectrum Disorder (ASD) support for neurodivergent children should focus on recognizing their unique talents and abilities. Many children on the spectrum have a remarkable ability to focus intensely on a particular subject or task. By providing opportunities for them to explore and develop their interests, parents can foster a sense of purpose and accomplishment in their child's life.

Attention Deficit Hyperactivity Disorder (ADHD) resources for neurodivergent children often emphasize their high energy levels and capacity for multitasking. While it may be challenging for them to concentrate for long periods, their ability to process information rapidly and multitask can be an advantage in certain situations. By harnessing these strengths, parents can help their ADHD children thrive in environments where quick thinking and adaptability are valued.

Sensory processing disorder interventions for neurodivergent children should focus on creating a sensory-friendly environment that allows them to explore and engage with their surroundings comfortably. Many neurodivergent children have heightened senses, which can provide them with a unique perspective on the world. By providing appropriate sensory experiences and accommodations, parents can help their children embrace their sensory strengths and navigate their environment with confidence.

Navigating Neurodiversity: A Guide for Parents of Neurodivergent Children

Learning disabilities assistance for neurodivergent children should prioritize identifying their individual learning styles and strengths. While they may struggle in certain areas, they may excel in others. By incorporating their strengths into their learning strategies, parents can help their children overcome challenges and achieve academic success.

Executive functioning skills development for neurodivergent children should focus on building organizational and time management skills while acknowledging their ability to think outside the box. Many neurodivergent children possess exceptional problem- solving abilities and creativity. By nurturing these strengths and providing support in areas of weakness, parents can help their children develop essential executive functioning skills.

Social skills training for neurodivergent children should emphasize their unique perspectives and abilities to connect with others. While they may struggle with social cues or communication, they often possess deep empathy and honesty. By fostering their strengths in building genuine connections and understanding emotions, parents can help their children develop meaningful relationships.

Emotional regulation strategies for neurodivergent children should recognize their heightened emotional sensitivity. Many neurodivergent children experience emotions intensely, which can be both challenging and advantageous. By teaching them healthy coping mechanisms and validating their emotions, parents can help them navigate their emotions and develop resilience.

Speech and language therapy for neurodivergent children should focus on their exceptional linguistic abilities. Many neurodivergent children have a unique way of processing and understanding language. By providing speech and language therapy that harnesses their strengths, parents can help their children communicate effectively and express themselves confidently.

Occupational therapy for neurodivergent children should consider their sensory preferences and strengths. Many neurodivergent children have a heightened sense of touch, taste, or smell, which can be incorporated into their occupational therapy sessions. By providing sensory-rich activities and accommodations, parents can help their children develop essential motor skills and achieve independence.

Parenting strategies for raising neurodivergent children should prioritize recognizing and celebrating their strengths. By focusing on their abilities rather than their disabilities, parents can create an environment that fosters growth and self-esteem. It is essential to remember that neurodivergent children have unique gifts to offer the world, and it is our role as parents to support and nurture these strengths.

In conclusion, recognizing and embracing the strengths of neurodivergent children is crucial for their overall development and self-esteem. By understanding their unique perspectives, abilities, and talents, parents can create an environment that celebrates neurodiversity and helps their children thrive.

Challenging Stereotypes and Misconceptions

Navigating Neurodiversity: A Guide for Parents of Neurodivergent Children

In our society, there are many stereotypes and misconceptions surrounding neurodivergent children. These stereotypes can lead to misunderstandings, exclusion, and limited opportunities for our children. However, it is essential for parents to challenge these stereotypes and misconceptions, as it is crucial for the well-being and success of our neurodivergent children.

One common misconception is that neurodivergent children are not capable of achieving success or leading fulfilling lives. This belief is not only false but also harmful to our children's self-esteem and motivation. Neurodivergent children have unique strengths and talents that should be celebrated and nurtured. By challenging this misconception, parents can help their children explore their interests and develop their abilities, ultimately empowering them to reach their full potential.

Another stereotype is that neurodivergent children are disruptive or difficult to manage. This misconception often leads to exclusion and stigmatization. However, it is crucial to understand that neurodivergent children are not intentionally disruptive but may struggle with certain aspects of their neurodivergence, such as sensory processing or executive functioning skills. By shifting our perspective and seeking appropriate interventions and support, parents can help their children navigate these challenges and thrive in various environments.

It is also important to challenge the belief that neurodivergent children do not have the same social and emotional needs as their neurotypical peers. Neurodivergent children may require additional support and strategies to develop social skills and regulate their emotions effectively. By providing targeted interventions and teaching these skills, parents can help their children build meaningful relationships and navigate social situations with confidence.

Furthermore, it is crucial to challenge the misconception that neurodivergent children's communication needs are the same as neurotypical children. Speech and language therapy can play a vital role in supporting neurodivergent children to communicate effectively. Occupational therapy can also provide valuable interventions to address sensory processing challenges and promote independence in daily activities.

In conclusion, challenging stereotypes and misconceptions is essential for parents of neurodivergent children. By advocating for their children's unique strengths, understanding their challenges, and seeking appropriate interventions and support, parents can help their children thrive and lead fulfilling lives. It is through this understanding and acceptance that we can create a more inclusive and supportive society for our neurodivergent children.

Chapter 2: Autism Spectrum Disorder (ASD) Support for Neurodivergent Children

Understanding Autism Spectrum Disorder

Autism Spectrum Disorder (ASD) is a complex neurodevelopmental condition that affects individuals in various ways. It is important for parents of neurodivergent children to have a clear understanding of ASD, as it can greatly impact their child's development and daily life.

ASD is characterized by challenges in social interaction, communication difficulties, and restricted and repetitive patterns of behavior. However, it is important to remember that ASD is a spectrum disorder, meaning that it affects individuals differently and to varying degrees. Some children with ASD may have mild symptoms and excel in certain areas, while others may require more support and have significant challenges.

Navigating Neurodiversity: A Guide for Parents of Neurodivergent Children

One of the key aspects of understanding ASD is recognizing the strengths and unique abilities of neurodivergent children. Many individuals with ASD have exceptional attention to detail, strong memory skills, and a unique way of thinking. By focusing on these strengths, parents can help their child develop strategies to navigate challenges and build on their abilities.

Support and resources are crucial for parents raising neurodivergent children with ASD. There are numerous interventions and therapies available that can help address specific needs. Speech and language therapy can assist with communication difficulties, while occupational therapy can provide strategies to improve sensory processing and motor skills. Additionally, social skills training can help children with ASD develop meaningful connections and navigate social interactions.

Parents can also play a crucial role in supporting their child's emotional regulation and executive functioning skills. By implementing parenting strategies that take into account their child's unique needs, parents can create a supportive and structured environment that promotes their child's development and well-being. This may include creating visual schedules, using social stories, and providing clear and consistent expectations.

Understanding ASD is a journey, and it is important for parents to seek out information, support, and resources to best support their child's needs. Navigating Neurodiversity: A Guide for Parents of Neurodivergent Children aims to provide parents with comprehensive information and practical strategies to help them navigate the challenges and celebrate the strengths of their neurodivergent child with ASD. By understanding and embracing the uniqueness of their child, parents can create a nurturing and empowering environment that allows their child to thrive.

Navigating Neurodiversity: A Guide for Parents of Neurodivergent Children

As parents, it is essential to recognize the early signs of neurodivergence in your child. Early intervention and diagnosis can greatly improve their quality of life and help them navigate the challenges they may face. In this subchapter, we will discuss the early signs and diagnosis of various neurodivergent conditions, including Autism Spectrum Disorder (ASD), Attention Deficit Hyperactivity Disorder (ADHD), sensory processing disorder, learning disabilities, and more.

Autism Spectrum Disorder (ASD) is a neurodevelopmental condition characterized by challenges in social interaction, communication, and restricted and repetitive behaviors. Some early signs of ASD may include delayed speech or language skills, difficulty making eye contact, repetitive movements, and a lack of interest in social interactions. If you notice these signs in your child, it is important to seek a professional evaluation from a pediatrician or developmental specialist.

Attention Deficit Hyperactivity Disorder (ADHD) is another common neurodivergent condition that affects children's ability to pay attention, control impulses, and regulate their behavior. Symptoms of ADHD can vary, but some early signs may include difficulty staying focused, excessive fidgeting, impulsivity, and trouble following instructions.
Consulting with a medical professional or a child psychologist can help determine whether your child may have ADHD and guide you towards appropriate resources and interventions.

Navigating Neurodiversity: A Guide for Parents of Neurodivergent Children

Sensory processing disorder refers to difficulties in processing sensory information, such as touch, sound, taste, and smell. Children with sensory processing disorder may be oversensitive or under sensitive to certain stimuli, leading to challenges in daily functioning. Signs of sensory processing disorder can include extreme reactions to certain textures, sounds, or smells, as well as difficulty with transitions. Seeking guidance from an occupational therapist who specializes in sensory processing can provide valuable strategies and interventions for your child.

Learning disabilities encompass a range of conditions that affect a child's ability to acquire and use academic skills effectively. If your child is struggling with reading, writing, math, or other academic tasks despite adequate instruction, it may be an indication of a learning disability. A comprehensive evaluation by a learning specialist or educational psychologist can help identify specific learning challenges and guide you towards appropriate interventions and accommodations.

Early diagnosis and intervention are crucial for neurodivergent children to thrive. By being aware of the early signs and seeking professional guidance, parents can access the necessary resources and support to help their children develop essential skills, such as executive functioning, social skills, emotional regulation, speech and language, and occupational therapy. Additionally, implementing effective parenting strategies tailored to the unique needs of neurodivergent children can create a nurturing and supportive environment that fosters their growth and development. Remember, you are not alone in this journey, and with proper support, your child can navigate neurodiversity with confidence and resilience.

Creating an Autism-Friendly Environment

Navigating Neurodiversity: A Guide for Parents of Neurodivergent Children

When it comes to supporting our neurodivergent children, creating an autism-friendly environment is essential. Autism Spectrum Disorder (ASD) affects individuals in various ways, making it crucial to tailor our surroundings to meet their unique needs. By doing so, we can help our children thrive and reach their full potential. In this subchapter, we will delve into practical strategies and interventions that can be implemented to foster an autism-friendly environment.

First and foremost, it is essential to understand the sensory processing challenges that many neurodivergent children face. Sensory processing disorder can greatly impact their ability to navigate their surroundings comfortably. Consider providing a calm and quiet space where your child can retreat when feeling overwhelmed. This might include using noise-cancelling headphones or creating a sensory-friendly corner with soft lighting and comfortable seating.

In addition to sensory needs, it is crucial to address executive functioning skills. Many neurodivergent children struggle with organization, planning, and time management. Implement visual schedules and checklists to help them stay on track and provide clear expectations. Break down tasks into smaller, manageable steps to promote success and reduce frustration.

Social skills training is another vital aspect of creating an autism-friendly environment. Many neurodivergent children struggle with social interactions and friendships.
Encourage opportunities for socialization and provide support through social skills groups or therapy. Encouraging empathy and understanding among peers can also help create a more inclusive environment.

Emotional regulation strategies are essential for neurodivergent children, particularly those with ADHD or autism. Teach and model coping techniques such as deep breathing, mindfulness exercises, or sensory tools like stress balls. Encourage open communication and provide a safe space for your child to express their emotions without judgment.

Speech and language therapy and occupational therapy are valuable resources for neurodivergent children. These therapies can address communication difficulties and enhance fine motor skills, respectively. Collaborate with professionals in these fields to ensure your child receives the appropriate interventions and support.

Lastly, as parents, it is crucial to adopt effective parenting strategies when raising neurodivergent children. Educate yourself about your child's specific needs and seek out support networks or parenting groups. Developing a strong support system can provide guidance and encouragement throughout your journey.

Creating an autism-friendly environment requires a thoughtful and individualized approach. By addressing sensory needs, executive functioning skills, social interactions, emotional regulation, therapy interventions, and parenting strategies, we can cultivate an environment that supports our neurodivergent children and allows them to thrive.

Effective Communication Strategies

Communication plays a crucial role in the development and well-being of neurodivergent children. As a parent, understanding and implementing effective communication strategies can greatly enhance your child's ability to express themselves, connect with others, and navigate the world around them. In this subchapter, we will explore various communication strategies that are tailored to the unique needs of neurodivergent children.

Navigating Neurodiversity: A Guide for Parents of Neurodivergent Children

1. Clear and Concise Language: When communicating with your child, use simple and direct language. Avoid using complex sentences or idioms that may confuse them. Break down information into smaller, manageable parts to ensure comprehension.

2. Visual Supports: Many neurodivergent children benefit from visual supports to aid their communication. Utilize visual schedules, social stories, and visual cues to help them understand and follow instructions. This can enhance their ability to anticipate and navigate daily routines.

3. Social Skills Training: Neurodivergent children may struggle with social interactions. Engage them in social skills training programs that teach appropriate communication, turn-taking, and understanding non-verbal cues. Role-playing and peer modeling can be effective tools for practicing and reinforcing these skills.

4. Active Listening: Practice active listening by giving your child your full attention when they are speaking. Maintain eye contact, nod, and provide verbal cues to show that you are engaged in the conversation. This encourages your child to communicate openly and feel valued.

5. Visual Cues for Emotions: Many neurodivergent children find it challenging to identify and express their emotions. Use visual cues such as emotion charts or facial expression cards to help them recognize and label their feelings. This can support emotional regulation and communication.

6. Augmentative and Alternative Communication (AAC): For children who struggle with verbal communication, AAC systems such as picture exchange communication or assistive technology devices can be invaluable. These tools enable them to express their thoughts and needs effectively.

7. Collaborate with Professionals: Work closely with speech and language therapists, occupational therapists, and other professionals to develop personalized communication strategies for your child. These experts can provide insights, resources, and interventions tailored to their specific needs.

Remember, effective communication is a journey that requires patience, understanding, and flexibility. Each child is unique, and what works for one may not work for another. By implementing these strategies and seeking professional guidance, you are empowering your child to navigate neurodiversity with confidence and resilience.

Developing Social Skills in Children with ASD

One of the key challenges that parents of neurodivergent children, particularly those with Autism Spectrum Disorder (ASD), face is helping their children develop social skills. Social interactions can be overwhelming and confusing for children with ASD, but with the right strategies and support, they can learn to navigate social situations more effectively.

One important aspect of supporting social skills development in children with ASD is providing opportunities for social interaction. This can be done through structured playdates, social skills groups, or joining community programs specifically designed for neurodivergent children. These settings allow children to practice their social skills in a safe and supportive environment.

Another effective approach is using visual supports to aid in social understanding. Visual schedules, social stories, and visual cues can help children with ASD understand social expectations and navigate social situations more successfully. These visual supports can be used at home, school, or in any social setting to provide guidance and clarity.

It is also crucial to teach and reinforce specific social skills. This can include teaching children how to initiate and maintain conversations, take turns, share, and show empathy. Role-playing and modeling appropriate social behaviors can be helpful in teaching these skills. Consistency and repetition are key in reinforcing these skills and helping children generalize them to different contexts.

In addition to direct skill-building activities, it is important to address any underlying issues that may impact social skills development. Many children with ASD may also have co-occurring conditions such as Attention Deficit Hyperactivity Disorder (ADHD), sensory processing disorder, or learning disabilities. Addressing these issues through appropriate interventions, such as occupational therapy or speech and language therapy, can significantly support social skills development.

Parenting strategies are also essential in fostering social skills development in children with ASD. This can involve creating a structured and predictable environment, setting clear expectations, and providing positive reinforcement for appropriate social behaviors. It is important for parents to be patient, understanding, and supportive, while also encouraging their child's independence and growth.

Ultimately, developing social skills in children with ASD requires a multi-faceted approach that addresses the unique needs of each child. By providing opportunities for social interaction, using visual supports, teaching specific social skills, addressing co-occurring conditions, and implementing effective parenting strategies, parents can support their child's social development and help them thrive in social settings.

Chapter 3: Attention Deficit Hyperactivity Disorder (ADHD) Resources for Neurodivergent Children

Understanding ADHD

ADHD, or Attention Deficit Hyperactivity Disorder, is a neurodevelopmental disorder that affects millions of children worldwide. It is characterized by difficulties with attention, hyperactivity, and impulsivity. Understanding ADHD is essential for parents of neurodivergent children, as it can provide insights into their child's behavior and help them navigate the challenges that come with it.

One of the key aspects to understand about ADHD is that it is a spectrum disorder, meaning that it can present differently in each child. Some children may exhibit primarily hyperactive and impulsive behaviors, while others may struggle more with inattentiveness. It is crucial for parents to recognize the unique characteristics of their child's ADHD and tailor interventions and support accordingly.

In diagnosing ADHD, it is important to consult with a healthcare professional who specializes in neurodevelopmental disorders. They will conduct a comprehensive evaluation, considering the child's behavior across multiple settings, such as home and school. This evaluation may involve interviews with parents and teachers, as well as behavioral assessments.

Navigating Neurodiversity: A Guide for Parents of Neurodivergent Children

Once a child is diagnosed with ADHD, parents can explore various resources and interventions to support their child's needs. These can include educational accommodations, such as specialized learning plans or classroom modifications. Occupational therapy and speech and language therapy can also be beneficial in addressing sensory processing issues and communication difficulties that often coexist with ADHD.

Parents can also focus on developing their child's executive functioning skills, which are essential for self-regulation, planning, and organization. This can be achieved through structured routines, visual supports, and teaching strategies that promote self- monitoring and problem-solving.

Social skills training is another important aspect of supporting neurodivergent children with ADHD. It can involve teaching specific social skills, such as turn-taking and active listening, as well as providing opportunities for social interaction with peers.

Emotional regulation strategies are crucial for children with ADHD, as they often struggle with managing their emotions. Parents can help their child develop these skills through techniques such as deep breathing exercises, mindfulness, and providing a calm and consistent environment.

Lastly, parenting strategies play a significant role in raising neurodivergent children with ADHD. This can include setting clear expectations, implementing positive reinforcement techniques, and using effective communication strategies. Seeking support from parent support groups or therapy can also be beneficial for parents as they navigate the challenges of raising a child with ADHD.

Understanding ADHD is a continuous process, and parents should stay informed about the latest research and interventions available. By gaining a deeper understanding of this neurodivergent condition, parents can provide their children with the necessary support and resources to thrive and reach their full potential.

Identifying ADHD Symptoms in Children

As parents of neurodivergent children, it is important to be aware of the various challenges that your child may face. One such challenge that many neurodivergent children experience is Attention Deficit Hyperactivity Disorder (ADHD). Recognizing the symptoms of ADHD in your child is crucial in order to provide them with the necessary support and interventions they may need. In this subchapter, we will discuss the key indicators of ADHD and provide resources and strategies for parents to navigate this aspect of neurodiversity.

ADHD is a neurodevelopmental disorder characterized by difficulties in sustaining attention, impulsivity, and hyperactivity. While it is normal for children to display these behaviors to some extent, it becomes a concern when they significantly impact a child's daily functioning. Some common symptoms of ADHD include:

1. Inattention: Children with ADHD may have trouble staying focused on tasks, frequently making careless mistakes and becoming easily distracted.

2. Hyperactivity: They may constantly fidget, squirm, or have difficulty staying still. They might also talk excessively and struggle with taking turns during conversations or games.

3. Impulsivity: Children with ADHD often act without thinking, interrupting others, and struggling with waiting for their turn.

It is essential to remember that ADHD manifests differently in each child. Some may primarily exhibit inattentive symptoms, while others may display more hyperactive or impulsive behaviors. It is also important to consider that ADHD can coexist with other neurodivergent conditions such as Autism Spectrum Disorder (ASD), learning disabilities, and sensory processing disorders.

When you suspect that your child may have ADHD, it is advisable to seek professional evaluation and diagnosis from a qualified healthcare provider or psychologist specializing in neurodiversity. They can conduct comprehensive assessments and provide appropriate interventions tailored to your child's specific needs.

In addition to professional support, there are numerous resources available to assist parents in supporting their neurodivergent children with ADHD. These resources include therapy options such as speech and language therapy, occupational therapy, and sensory processing disorder interventions. Additionally, parents can learn about executive functioning skills development, social skills training, emotional regulation strategies, and parenting strategies specifically designed for raising neurodivergent children.

By recognizing and understanding the symptoms of ADHD in your child, you can take proactive steps to support their unique needs. With the right resources and strategies, you can help your child thrive and reach their full potential, fostering a positive and inclusive environment for the entire family. Remember, you are not alone on this journey, and there are many resources and support networks available to assist you every step of the way.

Managing ADHD Behaviors at Home and School

When it comes to managing ADHD behaviors in neurodivergent children, it is crucial for parents to establish effective strategies both at home and in the school environment. By adopting a holistic approach that combines various interventions, parents can create a supportive and nurturing environment that helps their child thrive. In this subchapter, we will explore different strategies and resources available to parents, focusing on the specific challenges faced by neurodivergent children with ADHD.

One of the key aspects of managing ADHD behaviors is creating a structured routine. Establishing consistent schedules for daily activities, such as waking up, eating meals, and completing homework, can help children with ADHD feel more organized and in control. Providing visual aids, such as charts and calendars, can also assist in reinforcing the routine and promoting independence.

Another important aspect is implementing sensory processing disorder interventions. Many neurodivergent children with ADHD experience sensory challenges, which can lead to difficulties in focusing and regulating their emotions. By creating a sensory-friendly environment at home and collaborating with the school to provide sensory breaks and accommodations, parents can help their child better manage these challenges.

Additionally, supporting executive functioning skills development is crucial for neurodivergent children with ADHD. Parents can assist their child by breaking down tasks into smaller, manageable steps and providing visual or verbal prompts to stay on track. Teaching organizational skills, such as using planners or checklists, can also enhance their ability to plan, prioritize, and complete tasks successfully.

Furthermore, social skills training and emotional regulation strategies are vital for neurodivergent children with ADHD. Parents can work with therapists or utilize resources to help their child develop social skills, such as engaging in conversations, understanding nonverbal cues, and managing conflicts. Implementing strategies like deep breathing exercises or mindfulness techniques can also aid in controlling impulsivity and emotional outbursts.

Collaboration with professionals, such as speech and language therapists and occupational therapists, can further support neurodivergent children with ADHD. These professionals can provide specialized interventions to address specific challenges related to communication, sensory integration, and motor skills.

Lastly, parents should educate themselves about different parenting strategies specifically tailored for raising neurodivergent children. By understanding the unique needs and strengths of their child, parents can create an environment that fosters growth, resilience, and self-advocacy.

In conclusion, managing ADHD behaviors in neurodivergent children requires a comprehensive and multifaceted approach. By implementing strategies such as establishing routines, providing sensory accommodations, developing executive functioning skills, and supporting social and emotional well-being, parents can help their children thrive both at home and in school. Collaborating with professionals and staying informed about the latest resources and interventions is key to ensuring the best possible outcomes for their neurodivergent child.

Developing Organization and Time Management Skills

Navigating Neurodiversity: A Guide for Parents of Neurodivergent Children

One of the key challenges that parents of neurodivergent children face is helping their children develop organization and time management skills. This subchapter will provide practical strategies and resources for parents to support their child's executive functioning skills.

Executive functioning refers to a set of cognitive processes that enable individuals to plan, organize, and manage their time effectively. Neurodivergent children, such as those with Autism Spectrum Disorder (ASD), Attention Deficit Hyperactivity Disorder (ADHD), or learning disabilities, often struggle with executive functioning skills.

To help your child develop organization skills, create a structured and predictable environment. This can include setting up a daily routine, using visual schedules or checklists, and organizing their physical space. Teach your child how to break tasks into smaller, manageable chunks and prioritize them. Encourage them to use tools like calendars, planners, or digital apps to keep track of their assignments, appointments, and deadlines.

Time management skills can be developed through various techniques. Use visual timers or countdowns to help your child understand the passage of time. Break larger tasks into smaller time blocks and provide regular breaks to prevent overwhelming. Teach your child how to estimate and allocate time for different activities. Encourage them to practice self-monitoring and reflection on how they spend their time.

Navigating Neurodiversity: A Guide for Parents of Neurodivergent Children

There are numerous resources available to support neurodivergent children in developing organization and time management skills. Websites, books, and apps specifically designed for children with ASD, ADHD, and learning disabilities offer strategies, tools, and visual aids to enhance executive functioning. Speech and language therapy and occupational therapy can also address specific challenges related to organization and time management.

In addition to these interventions, it is crucial for parents to implement effective parenting strategies. Create a positive and supportive environment where mistakes are seen as opportunities for growth. Break tasks into smaller steps and provide clear instructions. Praise your child's efforts and progress, and offer specific feedback to reinforce desired behaviors.

By focusing on developing organization and time management skills, parents can empower their neurodivergent children to navigate their daily lives more independently and confidently. With patience, consistency, and the right resources, parents can help their children thrive and succeed in various domains of life.

Supporting Academic Success for Children with ADHD

Children with Attention Deficit Hyperactivity Disorder (ADHD) often face unique challenges when it comes to academic success. However, with the right support and strategies in place, parents can help their neurodivergent children thrive in the classroom and reach their full potential. This subchapter aims to provide parents with valuable resources and guidance on supporting the academic journey of their ADHD child.

Navigating Neurodiversity: A Guide for Parents of Neurodivergent Children

One of the key aspects of supporting academic success for children with ADHD is creating a structured and organized environment. Establishing routines, setting clear expectations, and maintaining a consistent schedule can help children with ADHD stay focused and on track. Additionally, creating a dedicated study space that is free from distractions can greatly enhance their ability to concentrate and complete schoolwork.

Another important consideration is providing appropriate interventions and accommodations. Working closely with teachers, parents can advocate for their child's needs in the classroom. This may include providing extra time for assignments and tests, allowing for movement breaks, or implementing visual aids to aid in comprehension. By working collaboratively with educators, parents can ensure that their child's unique learning style is supported.

Executive functioning skills development is crucial for children with ADHD. These skills involve planning, organization, time management, and self-regulation. Parents can help their child develop these skills through strategies such as breaking tasks into smaller, manageable steps, using visual schedules and reminders, and teaching self-monitoring techniques.

Social skills training is also essential for children with ADHD. These children may struggle with impulse control and maintaining appropriate social interactions. Parents can seek out social skills groups or therapy to help their child navigate social situations successfully.

Emotional regulation strategies play a significant role in supporting children with ADHD. Teaching self-calming techniques, such as deep breathing or journaling, can help children manage their emotions and reduce impulsivity.

Speech and language therapy and occupational therapy can also be valuable resources for children with ADHD. These therapies can address challenges in communication, sensory processing, and motor skills, which can affect academic performance.

Lastly, parents can benefit from learning effective parenting strategies for raising neurodivergent children. This may include utilizing positive reinforcement, setting clear boundaries, and practicing self-care to ensure they have the energy and patience needed to support their child's academic journey.

In conclusion, supporting academic success for children with ADHD requires a multi-faceted approach that addresses their specific needs. By providing structure, accommodations, interventions, and teaching essential skills, parents can empower their neurodivergent children to thrive academically and reach their full potential.

Chapter 4: Sensory Processing Disorder Interventions for Neurodivergent Children

Understanding Sensory Processing Disorder

Sensory Processing Disorder (SPD) is a neurological condition that affects how the brain processes and responds to sensory information from the environment. For parents of neurodivergent children, understanding SPD is crucial in providing effective support and interventions. This subchapter will delve into the various aspects of SPD and explore strategies to navigate this condition.

SPD can manifest in different ways and vary in severity among neurodivergent children. Some may be hypersensitive, reacting strongly to even mild sensory stimuli, while others may be hyposensitive, seeking out intense sensory experiences. These sensitivities can impact daily activities, including eating, dressing, and social interactions.

One of the key challenges faced by parents is identifying the signs of SPD in their child. Common signs include difficulty tolerating certain textures, sounds, or lights, avoiding or seeking out specific sensory experiences, poor coordination, and sensory seeking or avoiding behaviors. It is important to consult with a healthcare professional to obtain a proper diagnosis and develop a comprehensive treatment plan.

Interventions for SPD can significantly improve a child's quality of life. Occupational therapy (OT) is often recommended as it focuses on helping children develop and improve their sensory integration skills. OT sessions may involve activities that stimulate and regulate the child's sensory system, such as swinging, brushing, or deep pressure touch.

In addition to OT, other interventions such as speech and language therapy, social skills training, and executive functioning skills development can also be beneficial. These therapies aim to address specific challenges related to communication, social interactions, and cognitive abilities.

Emotional regulation strategies play a crucial role in supporting neurodivergent children with SPD. Teaching children coping techniques, such as deep breathing exercises or using sensory tools, can help them manage sensory overload and maintain emotional well-being.

As parents, it is important to educate ourselves about SPD and become advocates for our children. By understanding our child's sensory needs, we can make necessary adjustments at home, school, and in social settings to create a supportive environment. This may include providing sensory breaks, using visual schedules, or implementing sensory-friendly strategies.

Navigating SPD can be challenging, but with the right guidance and interventions, parents can help their neurodivergent children thrive. By fostering a holistic approach that addresses the sensory, cognitive, emotional, and social aspects of SPD, parents can empower their children to reach their full potential.

Recognizing Sensory Overload and Sensory Seeking Behaviors

One of the key challenges faced by parents of neurodivergent children is understanding and managing sensory overload and sensory seeking behaviors. These behaviors are commonly observed in children with conditions such as Autism Spectrum Disorder (ASD), Attention Deficit Hyperactivity Disorder (ADHD), sensory processing disorder, and learning disabilities. In this subchapter, we will explore these behaviors and provide strategies to support your child.

Sensory overload occurs when a child's brain receives more sensory information than it can effectively process. This can lead to feelings of overwhelm, anxiety, and even meltdowns. Common triggers for sensory overload include loud noises, bright lights, strong smells, and crowded environments. As a parent, it is important to recognize the signs of sensory overload in your child, which may include covering their ears, avoiding certain textures or fabrics, or becoming easily irritable. By identifying these triggers and creating a sensory-friendly environment, you can help your child cope with sensory overload. This may involve providing noise-canceling headphones, using dimmer lights, or creating calm spaces for your child to retreat to when they feel overwhelmed.

On the other hand, some neurodivergent children may engage in sensory seeking behaviors. These children actively seek out sensory stimulation as a way to regulate their nervous system. They may engage in repetitive movements like rocking or spinning, seek intense physical sensations, or have a heightened need for touch. It is important to understand that these behaviors are not disruptive or attention-seeking; rather, they serve a purpose by helping the child feel more grounded and focused. As a parent, you can support your child's sensory seeking needs by providing appropriate outlets for sensory input. This may include activities such as swinging, jumping on a trampoline, or using fidget toys.

Navigating sensory overload and sensory seeking behaviors requires a combination of understanding, patience, and proactive strategies. It is essential to work closely with your child's therapists and educators to develop a comprehensive plan that addresses their specific needs. Additionally, educating yourself about the different therapies and interventions available, such as speech and language therapy, occupational therapy, and social skills training, can empower you to make informed decisions about your child's development.

Remember, every child is unique, and what works for one may not work for another. By recognizing and addressing sensory overload and sensory seeking behaviors, you can create a supportive and nurturing environment that allows your neurodivergent child to thrive.

Creating a Sensory-Friendly Environment

Navigating Neurodiversity: A Guide for Parents of Neurodivergent Children

One of the key challenges faced by parents of neurodivergent children is creating a sensory-friendly environment that supports their child's unique needs. A sensory-friendly environment is crucial for children with neurodivergent conditions such as Autism Spectrum Disorder (ASD), Attention Deficit Hyperactivity Disorder (ADHD), sensory processing disorder, and learning disabilities. In this subchapter, we will explore effective strategies and interventions to help parents create a sensory-friendly environment for their neurodivergent children.

Firstly, it is important to understand the sensory sensitivities and triggers that affect your child. Pay close attention to their reactions to different sensory stimuli, such as loud noises, bright lights, strong smells, or certain textures. By identifying their specific triggers, you can modify their environment accordingly.

Start by creating a calming space within your home. This can be a designated area where your child can retreat to when they are feeling overwhelmed. Fill this space with sensory tools and equipment, such as weighted blankets, fidget toys, noise-cancelling headphones, or dimmable lights. These tools can help your child regulate their sensory input and maintain a sense of calm.

Consider making changes to your home environment to reduce sensory overload. For example, you can install blackout curtains to control the amount of light entering a room. Use soft, muted colors on the walls and avoid clutter, as a visually busy environment can be overwhelming for neurodivergent children.

Incorporate sensory activities into your child's daily routine. These can include activities such as finger painting, sensory bins, or playing with textured materials. By providing opportunities for sensory exploration, you can help your child develop their sensory processing skills and improve their overall sensory tolerance.

Collaborate with professionals such as occupational therapists, speech and language therapists, and learning specialists who can provide specific strategies and interventions tailored to your child's needs. They can offer guidance on how to create a sensory-friendly environment both at home and in other settings, such as school or community spaces.

Lastly, remember that each neurodivergent child is unique, and what works for one may not work for another. Be open to experimentation and adjust your strategies as needed. Regularly check in with your child to understand their sensory experiences and make adjustments accordingly.

Creating a sensory-friendly environment is an ongoing process, but with patience and persistence, you can provide your neurodivergent child with a supportive and nurturing environment that promotes their overall well-being and development.

Sensory Integration Techniques and Therapies

When it comes to supporting neurodivergent children, one crucial aspect to consider is their sensory integration. Sensory integration refers to the brain's ability to process and interpret information from our senses, such as touch, sight, sound, taste, and smell. For children with conditions like Autism Spectrum Disorder (ASD), Attention Deficit Hyperactivity Disorder (ADHD), sensory processing disorder, or learning disabilities, this process can be challenging. However, there are various techniques and therapies available to help them navigate their sensory experiences effectively.

Navigating Neurodiversity: A Guide for Parents of Neurodivergent Children

One of the most common approaches to sensory integration is occupational therapy (OT). In OT sessions, trained therapists work with children to develop strategies for managing sensory input and improving their sensory processing abilities. These sessions may include activities such as swinging, jumping, brushing, or playing with sensory toys to provide sensory input in a controlled and therapeutic manner. Occupational therapy can significantly benefit children by helping them regulate their responses to sensory stimuli and enhancing their overall sensory integration skills.

Speech and language therapy is another valuable resource for neurodivergent children. Many children with neurodiverse conditions struggle with speech and language development, which can further impact their ability to communicate effectively. Speech therapists use a variety of techniques, including visual aids, sign language, and augmentative and alternative communication (AAC) devices, to help children improve their communication skills. By addressing speech and language difficulties, this therapy contributes to better overall sensory integration and social interaction.

For parents, understanding and implementing effective parenting strategies is crucial. These strategies can include creating a structured and predictable environment, providing clear and concise instructions, and using visual supports to aid in communication and routine establishment. Additionally, parents can learn techniques for promoting emotional regulation, such as deep breathing exercises, mindfulness activities, and creating a calming sensory space at home.

In conclusion, sensory integration techniques and therapies play a vital role in supporting neurodivergent children. By addressing sensory challenges through occupational therapy, speech and language therapy, and incorporating effective parenting strategies, parents can help their children develop essential skills for sensory processing, communication, emotional regulation, and overall well-being. It is important to remember that every child is unique, and finding the right combination of interventions and support is crucial for their success. By seeking out appropriate resources and working closely with therapists and educators, parents can navigate the journey of raising neurodivergent children with confidence and provide them with the tools they need to thrive.

Chapter 5: Learning Disabilities Assistance for Neurodivergent Children

Understanding Learning Disabilities

In this subchapter, we will delve into the topic of learning disabilities and explore its impact on neurodivergent children. Learning disabilities refer to a range of disorders that affect a child's ability to acquire, process, and comprehend information. These difficulties can manifest in various areas such as reading, writing, math, and language skills. As parents of neurodivergent children, it is crucial to have a comprehensive understanding of learning disabilities to provide the necessary support and interventions.

Navigating Neurodiversity: A Guide for Parents of Neurodivergent Children

For neurodivergent children, such as those with Autism Spectrum Disorder (ASD), Attention Deficit Hyperactivity Disorder (ADHD), or sensory processing disorders, learning disabilities can further complicate their educational journey. Recognizing the signs and symptoms of learning disabilities is essential for early identification and intervention.

Some common indicators include struggling with reading comprehension, difficulties in spelling or writing, challenges with math concepts, and delayed language development.

When it comes to addressing learning disabilities in neurodivergent children, a multidisciplinary approach is often recommended. Collaborating with professionals such as speech and language therapists, occupational therapists, and learning specialists can provide valuable insights and interventions. These experts can help develop strategies to enhance executive functioning skills, improve social skills, and regulate emotions.

Parenting strategies play a crucial role in supporting and raising neurodivergent children with learning disabilities. Creating a structured and supportive environment, establishing clear routines, and providing individualized learning plans can greatly benefit their educational journey. Additionally, promoting self-advocacy skills and fostering a positive mindset can empower neurodivergent children to embrace their strengths and overcome challenges.

In this subchapter, we will explore various resources and interventions available for neurodivergent children with learning disabilities. From speech and language therapy to sensory processing disorder interventions, we will provide insights into each approach and its potential benefits. By arming yourself with knowledge and seeking appropriate support, you can help your child navigate the challenges posed by learning disabilities and empower them to reach their full potential.

Remember, every child is unique, and understanding their learning disabilities is the first step towards unlocking their true potential.

Identifying Different Types of Learning Disabilities

When it comes to neurodivergent children, it is crucial for parents to understand the various types of learning disabilities that their child may have. By identifying these disabilities, parents can seek appropriate interventions and support to help their child thrive. In this subchapter, we will explore the different types of learning disabilities commonly seen in neurodivergent children, including autism spectrum disorder (ASD), attention deficit hyperactivity disorder (ADHD), sensory processing disorder, and more.

Autism Spectrum Disorder (ASD) is a neurodevelopmental disorder that affects a child's ability to communicate and interact socially. It is important for parents to recognize the signs of ASD, such as difficulty with eye contact, repetitive behaviors, and challenges in social interactions. By seeking ASD-specific resources and support, parents can provide their child with the necessary tools to navigate the world effectively.

Attention Deficit Hyperactivity Disorder (ADHD) is another common learning disability among neurodivergent children. Children with ADHD often struggle with impulsivity, hyperactivity, and inattention. Understanding the symptoms of ADHD is crucial for parents, as it allows them to explore appropriate interventions such as behavioral therapy, medication, and organizational strategies to support their child's learning and development.

Sensory processing disorder is a condition that affects how the brain processes sensory information. Neurodivergent children with sensory processing disorder may be hypersensitive or hyposensitive to certain sensory stimuli. By identifying the specific sensory challenges their child faces, parents can seek out interventions such as occupational therapy to help their child regulate their sensory experiences and improve their overall functioning.

Furthermore, learning disabilities such as dyslexia, dyscalculia, and dysgraphia can significantly impact a neurodivergent child's academic performance. Recognizing the signs of these learning disabilities, such as difficulty reading, writing, or understanding mathematical concepts, is crucial for parents seeking appropriate assistance and interventions. They can explore resources such as specialized tutoring, assistive technology, and individualized education plans (IEPs) to support their child's learning journey.

In conclusion, identifying the different types of learning disabilities in neurodivergent children is essential for parents. By understanding the specific challenges their child faces, parents can seek out appropriate interventions and support, such as ASD-specific resources, ADHD strategies, sensory processing disorder interventions, and assistance for specific learning disabilities. With the right tools and strategies, parents can help their neurodivergent child reach their full potential and thrive in all aspects of life.

Individualized Education Plans (IEPs) and 504 Plans

As parents of neurodivergent children, it is crucial to understand the various resources and support systems available to ensure your child's success in their educational journey. Two important tools that can greatly assist in this process are Individualized Education Plans (IEPs) and 504 Plans.

An Individualized Education Plan (IEP) is a legally binding document that outlines the specific educational goals and accommodations for a student with special needs. It is designed to ensure that your child receives the necessary support and services to effectively access and participate in their education. IEPs are typically developed by a team consisting of parents, teachers, special education professionals, and other relevant individuals who have a deep understanding of your child's unique needs.

On the other hand, a 504 Plan is another form of support that focuses on providing accommodations and modifications to students who have a disability that substantially limits a major life activity. Unlike IEPs, 504 Plans do not require specialized instruction but provide necessary adjustments in the learning environment. These plans are developed by a team that includes parents, teachers, and other school personnel.

Both IEPs and 504 Plans can offer a wide range of supports tailored to your child's specific needs. These may include accommodations such as extended time for assignments or tests, preferential seating, visual aids, assistive technology, or specialized instruction. The ultimate goal of these plans is to create an inclusive and supportive learning environment that allows neurodivergent children to thrive academically, socially, and emotionally.

To ensure your child receives the appropriate support, it is important to actively participate in the development and review of their IEP or 504 Plan. Familiarize yourself with the specific goals, accommodations, and services outlined in the plan, and collaborate closely with your child's teachers and school administrators to monitor progress and make any necessary adjustments.

Additionally, it is essential to advocate for your child's needs throughout their educational journey. Stay informed about your rights as a parent, seek out support from advocacy groups, and connect with other parents who have similar experiences. By working together, we can ensure that our neurodivergent children receive the education and support they deserve.

In conclusion, Individualized Education Plans (IEPs) and 504 Plans are invaluable tools that can help meet the unique needs of neurodivergent children. By actively engaging in the development and implementation of these plans, parents can ensure that their child receives the necessary accommodations and support to excel in their education. Remember, you are not alone on this journey. Reach out, seek support, and advocate for your child's needs to create an inclusive and empowering educational experience.

Effective Teaching Strategies for Children with Learning Disabilities

When it comes to teaching children with learning disabilities, it is crucial to adopt effective strategies that cater to their specific needs. In this subchapter, we will explore various approaches that can help parents support their neurodivergent children in their educational journey.

1. Individualized Education Plans (IEPs): Collaborate with your child's school to develop an IEP, which outlines specific goals, accommodations, and modifications tailored to your child's learning needs. Regular meetings with teachers and therapists will ensure that the plan is effectively implemented.

2. Multi-sensory Techniques: Incorporate multi-sensory activities into your child's learning experience. For example, using visual aids, hands-on materials, and interactive technology can enhance their understanding and engagement.

3. Differentiated Instruction: Recognize that each child learns differently and adapt teaching methods accordingly. Provide various instructional approaches, such as visual, auditory, or kinesthetic, to accommodate their individual learning styles.

4. Break Tasks into Smaller Steps: Learning disabilities often make it challenging for children to process information. Breaking down tasks into smaller, manageable steps can help them grasp concepts more easily and build their confidence.

5. Assistive Technology: Utilize assistive technology tools, such as text-to-speech software or dictation apps, to support reading and writing skills. These tools can help bridge the gap between their abilities and educational expectations.

6. Positive Reinforcement: Celebrate your child's successes, no matter how small. Encouragement and positive reinforcement can motivate them to persevere through challenges and build a positive attitude towards learning.

7. Social Skills Training: Recognize the importance of social skills for your child's overall development. Seek resources and programs that provide specific training in social interactions, communication, and building relationships.

8. Emotional Regulation Strategies: Help your child develop strategies to manage their emotions effectively. Techniques like deep breathing, mindfulness exercises, or using visual cues can assist them in self-regulating their emotions and maintaining focus.

9. Collaboration with Therapists: Coordinate with speech and language therapists, occupational therapists, and other specialists to reinforce their therapy goals at home. Regular communication and consistent practice will enhance the effectiveness of their interventions.

10. Parenting Strategies: Educate yourself about your child's specific learning disability and seek support from other parents or support groups who are facing similar challenges. Implementing effective parenting strategies, such as setting realistic expectations, maintaining routines, and fostering a nurturing environment, can contribute to your child's overall well-being.

Remember, each child is unique, and it may take time to find the strategies that work best for your neurodivergent child. Be patient, persistent, and supportive throughout their educational journey. Together, we can help our children thrive and reach their full potential.

Supporting Homework and Study Skills

When it comes to neurodivergent children, homework and studying can often present unique challenges. However, with the right strategies and support, parents can help their children develop effective homework and study skills to enhance their learning experience. This subchapter will explore various techniques and resources that are specifically tailored to the needs of neurodivergent children, including those with Autism Spectrum Disorder (ASD), Attention Deficit Hyperactivity Disorder (ADHD), sensory processing disorders, learning disabilities, and more.

One key aspect of supporting homework and study skills is creating a structured and organized environment. This can include setting up a designated study area free from distractions, developing a consistent routine, and using visual schedules or checklists to help children stay focused and on track. Additionally, providing clear instructions and breaking down tasks into smaller, manageable steps can make assignments feel less overwhelming.

Navigating Neurodiversity: A Guide for Parents of Neurodivergent Children

For children with ASD, ADHD, or learning disabilities, it may be beneficial to incorporate alternative learning strategies. This can involve using visual aids, hands-on activities, or technology-based tools to reinforce concepts and improve comprehension. Additionally, providing additional time for assignments or implementing a modified curriculum can accommodate their individual needs.

Parents can also explore various interventions and therapies to support their child's specific challenges. Speech and language therapy can help improve communication skills, while occupational therapy can address sensory issues and fine motor skills.
Additionally, executive functioning skills development programs can assist with organization, planning, and time management.

Social skills and emotional regulation strategies are equally important for neurodivergent children. Parents can seek out social skills training programs or engage in activities that promote social interaction and emotional understanding. Teaching self-regulation techniques, such as deep breathing or mindfulness exercises, can also help children manage their emotions more effectively.

Lastly, this subchapter will provide parenting strategies and resources for raising neurodivergent children. This can include guidance on advocating for their child's needs within the educational system, collaborating with teachers and therapists, and fostering a supportive and inclusive home environment.

By implementing these strategies and accessing the appropriate resources, parents can empower their neurodivergent children to develop effective homework and study skills. Ultimately, this will not only enhance their academic success but also promote their overall well-being and self-confidence.

Chapter 6: Executive Functioning Skills Development for Neurodivergent Children

Understanding Executive Functioning Challenges

Executive functioning refers to a set of cognitive processes that are responsible for planning, organizing, problem-solving, and regulating behavior. These skills are crucial for success in various areas of life, including academics, social interactions, and daily tasks.

However, neurodivergent children, such as those with Autism Spectrum Disorder (ASD), Attention Deficit Hyperactivity Disorder (ADHD), sensory processing disorder, learning disabilities, and other developmental differences, often face challenges in executive functioning.

For parents, it is essential to understand the specific executive functioning challenges that their neurodivergent child may encounter. By gaining this understanding, parents can provide appropriate support and interventions to help their child thrive. Here are a few key points to consider when it comes to executive functioning challenges:

1. Planning and Organization: Many neurodivergent children struggle with creating and following through with plans, organizing their belongings, and managing time effectively. Parents can help by breaking tasks into smaller, manageable steps, providing visual schedules or checklists, and offering consistent routines.

2. Problem-Solving and Flexibility: Neurodivergent children may find it challenging to adapt to unexpected changes or solve problems independently. Parents can encourage problem-solving skills by discussing different strategies, teaching flexible thinking, and providing opportunities for decision-making.

3. Impulse Control and Emotional Regulation: Children with executive functioning challenges often struggle with impulse control, emotional regulation, and understanding social cues. Parents can support their child by teaching calming techniques, providing a safe space for emotional expression, and modeling appropriate behavior.

4. Memory and Attention: Many neurodivergent children have difficulties with memory and attention, making it hard to focus, remember instructions, or retain information. Parents can assist by using visual aids, incorporating multisensory learning strategies, and providing regular breaks to avoid overload.

5. Communication and Social Skills: Executive functioning challenges can affect a child's ability to initiate and maintain conversations, understand non-verbal cues, and navigate social situations. Speech and language therapy and social skills training can be beneficial in fostering communication and social competence.

6. Occupational Therapy: Occupational therapy can help neurodivergent children in developing skills related to fine motor coordination, sensory integration, self-regulation, and adaptive behaviors, all of which contribute to executive functioning abilities.

By recognizing and understanding these executive functioning challenges, parents can seek appropriate interventions and resources to support their neurodivergent child's development. Parenting strategies that focus on building executive functioning skills, promoting emotional regulation, and fostering social connections can go a long way in helping these children thrive. Remember, every child is unique, and finding what works best for your child may require patience and experimentation.

Improving Time Management and Organization Skills

Navigating Neurodiversity: A Guide for Parents of Neurodivergent Children

As parents of neurodivergent children, one of the key challenges you may face is helping your child develop effective time management and organization skills. Neurodivergent children, such as those with Autism Spectrum Disorder (ASD), Attention Deficit Hyperactivity Disorder (ADHD), sensory processing disorder, learning disabilities, or executive functioning difficulties, often struggle with these skills. However, with the right strategies and support, you can help your child overcome these challenges and improve their overall functioning.

One of the first steps in improving time management and organization skills is creating a structured and predictable environment. Establishing routines and schedules can provide a sense of stability and help your child understand what is expected of them.
Visual supports, such as visual schedules or calendars, can be particularly helpful for neurodivergent children who may struggle with abstract concepts of time. These tools can help them better understand and manage their daily activities and responsibilities.

Breaking tasks down into smaller, manageable steps is another effective strategy. Neurodivergent children often struggle with task initiation and may become overwhelmed by large projects. By breaking tasks into smaller, more manageable steps, you can help your child approach tasks more easily and avoid feeling overwhelmed.
Additionally, providing clear and specific instructions can further support their understanding and completion of tasks.

Using visual aids, such as checklists or color-coded systems, can also aid in organization and time management. These tools can help your child prioritize tasks, track progress, and stay focused. Additionally, incorporating timers or alarms can help your child manage their time more effectively and stay on track.

Collaboration with your child's educators and therapists is crucial in improving time management and organization skills. They can provide valuable insights and suggest individualized strategies to support your child's specific needs. For example, speech and language therapists can work on developing executive functioning skills, while occupational therapists can help with sensory processing and fine motor skills.

It is also important to teach your child self-regulation and emotional regulation strategies. Neurodivergent children often struggle with emotional regulation, which can impact their ability to manage time and stay organized. Teaching them techniques such as deep breathing, mindfulness, or self-calming strategies can help them regulate their emotions and stay focused on their tasks.

Lastly, as parents, it is essential to practice patience and understanding. Neurodivergent children may require extra time and support to develop these skills. Celebrate their progress, no matter how small, and provide encouragement and positive reinforcement along the way.

Improving time management and organization skills is a journey that requires ongoing support and practice. By implementing these strategies and seeking guidance from professionals, you can help your neurodivergent child develop the necessary skills to navigate their daily lives more effectively and increase their overall independence and success.

Enhancing Planning and Problem-Solving Abilities

In this subchapter, we will explore strategies and techniques to help enhance the planning and problem-solving abilities of neurodivergent children. These skills are crucial for their overall development and success in various aspects of life, including academics, social interactions, and daily routines. By equipping parents with effective tools and approaches, we aim to support the growth and progress of their neurodivergent children.

Planning and problem-solving abilities are often challenging for neurodivergent children, including those on the Autism Spectrum Disorder (ASD), with Attention Deficit Hyperactivity Disorder (ADHD), sensory processing disorder, learning disabilities, and other related conditions. However, with the right interventions and support, these skills can be strengthened, leading to improved independence and self-confidence.

One effective approach to enhance planning and problem-solving abilities is through executive functioning skills development. Executive functions refer to the cognitive processes that help individuals manage their thoughts, actions, and emotions. By focusing on executive functions such as organization, time management, and cognitive flexibility, parents can assist their children in developing strategies to plan and solve problems effectively.

Furthermore, social skills training plays a vital role in improving planning and problem- solving abilities. Neurodivergent children often struggle with social interactions and understanding social cues, which can impact their ability to plan and solve problems in social settings. By providing structured social skills training, parents can help their children navigate social situations and develop strategies for effective planning and problem-solving within social contexts.

Additionally, emotional regulation strategies can significantly contribute to enhancing planning and problem-solving abilities. Neurodivergent children may experience difficulties in managing their emotions, which can hinder their ability to think clearly and solve problems effectively. Teaching strategies such as deep breathing exercises, mindfulness techniques, and positive self-talk can help children regulate their emotions and improve their planning and problem-solving skills.

Speech and language therapy and occupational therapy are additional resources that can support the development of planning and problem-solving abilities in neurodivergent children. These therapies can address specific communication and sensory needs, providing children with the necessary tools to express themselves effectively and engage in problem-solving tasks.

Lastly, parenting strategies play a crucial role in raising neurodivergent children with enhanced planning and problem-solving abilities. By providing a supportive and structured environment, setting clear expectations, and fostering independence, parents can empower their children to develop and apply planning and problem-solving skills in their daily lives.

In conclusion, enhancing planning and problem-solving abilities is essential for the overall development and success of neurodivergent children. By utilizing various interventions such as executive functioning skills development, social skills training, emotional regulation strategies, therapy resources, and effective parenting strategies, parents can support their children in building these skills and navigating neurodiversity with confidence and resilience.

Developing Self-Monitoring and Self-Regulation Skills

Navigating Neurodiversity: A Guide for Parents of Neurodivergent Children

One of the most important skills that neurodivergent children can develop is self-monitoring and self-regulation. These skills are crucial for their overall well-being and success in various areas of life. In this subchapter, we will explore strategies and techniques that parents can use to help their neurodivergent children develop these skills.

Self-monitoring involves the ability to observe and recognize one's own behaviors, emotions, and thoughts. It is the foundation upon which self-regulation is built. By becoming aware of their own actions and reactions, neurodivergent children can learn to modify and control their behavior in different situations.

To start developing self-monitoring skills, it is essential for parents to create a safe and supportive environment where their children feel comfortable exploring and expressing their emotions. Encourage open communication and provide opportunities for self-reflection. For example, ask your child how they felt during a particular activity and why they think they felt that way.

Once self-monitoring skills are established, the focus can shift to self-regulation. Self-regulation refers to the ability to control and manage one's own emotions, behaviors, and impulses. This skill is particularly important for neurodivergent children who may struggle with impulsivity or emotional dysregulation.

There are several strategies that parents can use to help their children develop self-regulation skills. One effective technique is the use of visual supports, such as visual schedules or emotion charts. These tools can help neurodivergent children understand and anticipate their routines, as well as identify and express their emotions.

Another helpful strategy is to teach children calming techniques, such as deep breathing or progressive muscle relaxation. These techniques can help neurodivergent children regulate their emotions and reduce stress or anxiety in challenging situations.

It is also important to provide consistent structure and routines for neurodivergent children. Predictability can help them feel more secure and in control, which in turn promotes self-regulation. Establish clear expectations and rules, and provide positive reinforcement when your child demonstrates self-regulatory behaviors.

Finally, remember that developing self-monitoring and self-regulation skills is a gradual process. Be patient and provide ongoing support and guidance to your neurodivergent child. Celebrate their progress and encourage their efforts, as even small steps towards self-regulation can make a significant difference in their lives.

By helping your neurodivergent child develop these skills, you are equipping them with tools that will enable them to navigate the challenges they may face. With self- monitoring and self-regulation, they can better manage their emotions, behaviors, and interactions with others.

Chapter 7: Social Skills Training for Neurodivergent Children

Understanding the Importance of Social Skills

Navigating Neurodiversity: A Guide for Parents of Neurodivergent Children

In the journey of raising neurodivergent children, it is essential for parents to recognize the importance of social skills development. Neurodivergent children, including those with Autism Spectrum Disorder (ASD), Attention Deficit Hyperactivity Disorder (ADHD), sensory processing disorder, learning disabilities, and other challenges, often face difficulties in navigating social interactions. However, with proper support and interventions, these children can thrive and build meaningful connections.

Social skills lay the foundation for successful relationships, communication, and overall well-being. By understanding the significance of social skills for neurodivergent children, parents can actively seek out resources and strategies to help their children develop these crucial abilities.

One of the key benefits of social skills training is improved social interaction. Neurodivergent children may struggle with understanding social cues, initiating conversations, or maintaining appropriate eye contact. By providing targeted social skills training, parents can equip their children with the tools to navigate these challenges effectively. This training can include role-playing scenarios, social stories, and direct instruction on social norms and expectations.

In addition to social interaction, social skills are vital for emotional regulation. Many neurodivergent children struggle with managing their emotions, leading to meltdowns or emotional outbursts. By developing social skills, children can learn to recognize and express their emotions in a more adaptive manner. They can also acquire strategies for self-soothing and calming themselves during stressful situations.

Furthermore, social skills are closely linked to executive functioning skills. Executive functioning encompasses abilities such as organization, planning, and problem-solving. By enhancing social skills, parents can indirectly support the development of executive functioning skills. For instance, engaging in social activities can help children practice time management, decision-making, and flexible thinking.

It is important to note that social skills development is not a one-size-fts-all approach. Each neurodivergent child is unique, and their social needs may vary. Therefore, parents should consider seeking professional guidance from speech and language therapists, occupational therapists, and other specialists who can provide individualized interventions tailored to their child's specific challenges.

In conclusion, understanding the importance of social skills is crucial for parents of neurodivergent children. By prioritizing social skills development, parents can empower their children to thrive in social interactions, regulate their emotions effectively, and strengthen executive functioning skills. With the right support, neurodivergent children can build meaningful connections and lead fulfilling lives.

Teaching Social Skills at Home and School

One of the key challenges faced by parents of neurodivergent children is helping them develop and navigate social skills. Neurodivergent children, including those with Autism Spectrum Disorder (ASD), Attention Deficit Hyperactivity Disorder (ADHD), sensory processing disorder, learning disabilities, and executive functioning difficulties, often struggle with social interactions and communication. However, with the right strategies and interventions, parents can support their children in developing essential social skills both at home and in a school setting.

First and foremost, it is crucial for parents to understand their child's unique needs and challenges. Each neurodivergent child is different, and what works for one may not necessarily work for another. By seeking professional advice and understanding their child's individual strengths and weaknesses, parents can tailor their approach to teaching social skills accordingly.

At home, parents can create a supportive environment that encourages social interaction and communication. This can be achieved by providing structured routines, visual schedules, and clear expectations. Engaging in activities that promote social skills, such as playing board games, role-playing, or participating in group activities, can also be beneficial.

In a school setting, collaboration with teachers and other professionals is essential. Parents can work together with educators to develop individualized education plans (IEPs) or behavior intervention plans (BIPs) that focus on social skill development. This may include strategies such as social stories, visual supports, peer modeling, and social skills groups.

Furthermore, seeking out additional resources and therapies can significantly support social skills development. Speech and language therapy can aid in improving communication skills, while occupational therapy can address sensory processing difficulties that can impact social interactions. Parents can also explore social skills training programs or workshops specifically designed for neurodivergent children.

Emotional regulation is another vital aspect of social skills development. Parents can teach their children strategies to identify and manage their emotions, such as deep breathing exercises, mindfulness techniques, and utilizing visual cues. It is crucial for parents to model and reinforce these strategies consistently, both at home and in the school environment.

Lastly, parenting strategies play a significant role in raising neurodivergent children with strong social skills. This may involve employing positive reinforcement, setting clear boundaries, and using visual supports to enhance understanding and compliance.
Seeking support from other parents who are navigating similar challenges can also provide valuable insights and a sense of community.

Teaching social skills to neurodivergent children requires patience, understanding, and a willingness to adapt strategies as needed. By creating a supportive and inclusive environment at home and collaborating with educators and professionals, parents can empower their children to thrive socially and build meaningful relationships.

Building Friendships and Peer Relationships

One of the key challenges that neurodivergent children face is developing and maintaining friendships and peer relationships. Neurodivergent children, such as those with Autism Spectrum Disorder (ASD), Attention Deficit Hyperactivity Disorder (ADHD), sensory processing disorder, learning disabilities, and executive functioning difficulties, often struggle with social interactions and may find it difficult to connect with their peers. As parents, it is crucial to understand and support your child in building these important relationships.

Here are some strategies and resources to help you navigate the journey of building friendships and peer relationships for your neurodivergent child:

Navigating Neurodiversity: A Guide for Parents of Neurodivergent Children

1. **Social Skills Training:** Consider enrolling your child in social skills training programs specifically designed for neurodivergent children. These programs focus on teaching essential social skills, such as initiating conversations, sharing, turn-taking, and understanding nonverbal cues. They provide a safe and supportive environment for children to practice and improve their social interactions.

2. **Peer Support Groups:** Look for local support groups or community organizations that offer peer support for neurodivergent children. These groups provide an opportunity for your child to meet others facing similar challenges, share experiences, and develop meaningful friendships.

3. **Emotional Regulation Strategies:** Help your child develop strategies to manage their emotions effectively. This might include teaching them deep breathing exercises, mindfulness techniques, or using visual supports to identify and express their feelings. When children can regulate their emotions, they are better equipped to form and maintain positive relationships with their peers.

4. **Speech and Language Therapy:** If your child struggles with communication, consider seeking speech and language therapy. A speech-language pathologist can work with your child to improve their language skills, including verbal and nonverbal communication, which can enhance their ability to connect with others.

5. **Parenting Strategies:** As a parent, you play a crucial role in supporting your child's social development. Learn about effective parenting strategies, such as positive reinforcement, modeling appropriate social behaviors, and providing structure and routine. These strategies can help create a supportive and nurturing environment for your child to thrive socially.

Remember, building friendships and peer relationships takes time and patience. Encourage your child to participate in activities they enjoy, such as clubs, sports teams, or arts programs, where they can meet like-minded peers. Celebrate their successes and provide support when they face challenges. By actively supporting and advocating for your neurodivergent child, you can help them develop meaningful connections and friendships that will positively impact their overall well-being.

Navigating Social Challenges and Bullying

Introduction:

One of the most significant challenges that neurodivergent children face is navigating social situations and dealing with bullying. As a parent of a neurodivergent child, it is essential to equip yourself with the knowledge and strategies to support your child through these difficulties. This subchapter aims to provide guidance and resources to help you understand and address social challenges and bullying effectively.

Understanding Social Challenges:

Neurodivergent children often struggle with understanding social cues, maintaining eye contact, interpreting body language, and engaging in reciprocal conversations. These challenges can lead to social isolation, feelings of loneliness, and vulnerability to bullying. It is crucial for parents to recognize and empathize with their child's difficulties in social interactions.

Identifying Bullying:

Bullying can have a detrimental impact on neurodivergent children's mental health and self-esteem. It is vital for parents to be vigilant and able to identify signs of bullying in their child's behavior. These signs may include sudden changes in mood, withdrawal from social activities, unexplained injuries, or a decline in academic performance. By being aware of these indicators, parents can take prompt action to address the issue.

Supporting Your Child:

There are various strategies and resources available to support neurodivergent children in navigating social challenges and bullying. Seek out support groups, online communities, and local organizations that provide guidance specifically tailored to the needs of neurodivergent children and their parents. These resources can offer advice, share personal experiences, and offer strategies to help your child develop social skills and cope with bullying.

Working with Professionals:

Collaborating with professionals such as therapists, counselors, and educators can be immensely helpful in addressing social challenges and bullying. Speech and language therapists can assist in developing communication skills, while occupational therapists can provide strategies for sensory processing issues. Additionally, professionals specializing in ADHD and learning disabilities can offer interventions and accommodations to support your child's social development.

Parenting Strategies:

As a parent of a neurodivergent child, it is crucial to implement effective parenting strategies to promote social skills development and resilience. Encourage open communication, actively listen to your child's concerns, and provide a safe and supportive environment. Teach your child about self-advocacy, problem-solving, and assertiveness skills to empower them in social situations.

Conclusion:

Navigating social challenges and bullying can be particularly challenging for neurodivergent children. However, with the right knowledge, resources, and support, parents can help their children develop social skills, overcome adversity, and thrive. By implementing effective parenting strategies and seeking professional guidance, parents can ensure that their neurodivergent children feel supported, understood, and equipped to face the social world with confidence.

Chapter 8: Emotional Regulation Strategies for Neurodivergent Children

Understanding Emotional Regulation Difficulties

Emotional regulation is a critical aspect of our daily lives, enabling us to navigate and respond appropriately to the myriad of emotions we experience. However, for neurodivergent children, such as those with Autism Spectrum Disorder (ASD), Attention Deficit Hyperactivity Disorder (ADHD), sensory processing disorder, learning disabilities, and other related conditions, emotional regulation can pose significant challenges. In this subchapter, we will explore the various aspects of emotional regulation difficulties and provide strategies to support your neurodivergent child.

Neurodivergent children often struggle with identifying and labeling their emotions accurately. They may experience intense emotions but lack the necessary skills to express or regulate them effectively. This can lead to meltdowns, outbursts, or emotional shutdowns, which can be distressing for both the child and the parent. Understanding the underlying causes of these difficulties is crucial in devising effective interventions.

One common factor contributing to emotional regulation difficulties in neurodivergent children is sensory processing issues. Sensory overload or sensitivity can overwhelm a child's emotional capacity, making it harder for them to regulate their emotions. By implementing sensory interventions, such as creating sensory-friendly environments or providing sensory breaks, parents can help their children find balance and regulate their emotions more effectively.

Another key contributor to emotional regulation difficulties is executive functioning deficits. These deficits can impair a child's ability to plan, organize, and manage their emotions. Parents can support their children by developing executive functioning skills through strategies such as visual schedules, task breakdowns, and teaching problem- solving techniques.

Additionally, social skills deficits can impact emotional regulation. Neurodivergent children may struggle with understanding social cues, interpreting others' emotions, and appropriately responding in social situations. Social skills training programs can be beneficial in teaching these skills and enabling children to better regulate their emotions in social contexts.

Speech and language therapy and occupational therapy can also play a crucial role in supporting emotional regulation. These therapies can help children develop communication skills, self-expression, and sensory integration, which are all essential components of emotional regulation.

Lastly, as parents, it is essential to employ effective parenting strategies that promote emotional regulation in neurodivergent children. This includes establishing consistent routines, providing clear expectations, implementing positive reinforcement, and fostering a supportive and empathetic environment.

Understanding and addressing emotional regulation difficulties is vital for the overall well-being and development of neurodivergent children. By utilizing the strategies and interventions outlined in this subchapter, parents can provide the necessary support to help their children navigate and regulate their emotions more effectively. With patience,
understanding, and targeted interventions, we can empower neurodivergent children to develop the emotional regulation skills they need to thrive.

Teaching Emotional Awareness and Expression

In the journey of raising neurodivergent children, one crucial aspect that requires special attention is their emotional awareness and expression. Neurodivergent children, including those with Autism Spectrum Disorder (ASD), Attention Deficit Hyperactivity Disorder (ADHD), learning disabilities, and sensory processing disorders, often face challenges in understanding and managing their emotions. As parents, it is essential to provide them with the necessary tools and support to navigate these complexities.

Navigating Neurodiversity: A Guide for Parents of Neurodivergent Children

Emotional awareness is the ability to recognize and understand one's own emotions and the emotions of others. It lays the foundation for effective emotional expression and regulation. By teaching our neurodivergent children emotional awareness, we empower them to communicate their feelings, navigate social interactions, and develop healthy relationships.

One effective strategy to teach emotional awareness is through visual aids. Many neurodivergent children, especially those with ASD or ADHD, benefit from using visual supports such as emotion charts, social stories, or emotion cards. These tools help them identify and label different emotions, facilitating their understanding and expression.

Another valuable approach is the use of social skills training. Neurodivergent children often struggle with social interactions, which can impact their emotional well-being. By providing them with targeted social skills training, we can enhance their ability to recognize and respond appropriately to social cues, manage conflict, and build meaningful connections with others.

To support emotional regulation in neurodivergent children, it is crucial to teach them coping strategies. These can include deep breathing exercises, sensory breaks, or engaging in activities that provide a sense of calm and relaxation. By equipping them with these strategies, we empower them to self-regulate and manage their emotions effectively.

Speech and language therapy and occupational therapy also play a vital role in teaching emotional awareness and expression. These therapies focus on developing communication skills, enhancing sensory processing, and promoting self-expression.
Through these interventions, neurodivergent children can improve their ability to express their emotions verbally and non-verbally.

Navigating Neurodiversity: A Guide for Parents of Neurodivergent Children

As parents, it is essential to adopt specific parenting strategies that foster emotional growth in our neurodivergent children. This includes creating a safe and supportive environment, promoting open communication, and validating their emotions. By actively listening and empathizing with their experiences, we establish a foundation of trust and emotional connection.

Navigating the emotional landscape of neurodivergent children can be challenging, but by teaching emotional awareness and expression, we equip them with invaluable life skills. With our guidance, they can develop a better understanding of their emotions, express themselves effectively, and thrive in their personal and social lives.

Coping Strategies for Managing Strong Emotions

As parents of neurodivergent children, one of the most challenging aspects we face is helping our children manage their strong emotions. Whether it's a meltdown, an outburst of anger, or extreme anxiety, these intense emotions can be overwhelming for both the child and the parent. However, there are coping strategies that can help us navigate these situations and support our children in regulating their emotions.

1. Recognize and Validate Emotions: The first step is to acknowledge and validate your child's emotions. Let them know that it's okay to feel angry, sad, or anxious. By validating their emotions, you create a safe space for them to express themselves.

2. Teach Emotional Literacy: Help your child understand and label their emotions by using visual aids, such as emotion charts or mood cards. Encourage them to express how they feel in words, as this can enhance their emotional intelligence and communication skills.

3. **Create a Calming Environment:** Designate a quiet and cozy space in your home where your child can retreat when they feel overwhelmed. Fill this space with comforting items like soft pillows, sensory toys, or calming music. This can provide them with a safe haven to relax and regain control.

4. **Teach Deep Breathing Techniques:** Deep breathing exercises can help your child calm their nervous system during moments of heightened emotions. Practice deep breathing together and encourage them to use this technique whenever they feel overwhelmed.

5. **Use Visual Supports:** Visual supports, such as visual schedules, social stories, or emotion thermometers, can help your child understand what to expect and how to manage their emotions in different situations. These visuals provide a concrete framework that can reduce anxiety and promote self-regulation.

6. **Engage in Sensory Activities:** Sensory activities, such as swinging, jumping on a trampoline, or playing with sensory bins, can help your child release pent-up emotions and regulate their sensory system. Experiment with different sensory experiences to find what works best for your child.

7. **Seek Professional Support:** Consider seeking professional support from therapists specializing in neurodivergent children. Speech and language therapy, occupational therapy, and social skills training can provide valuable tools and strategies tailored to your child's specific needs.

Remember, coping strategies take time and practice. Be patient with yourself and your child as you navigate this journey together. Celebrate small victories and seek support from other parents who understand your unique challenges. By implementing these coping strategies, you can empower your child to manage their strong emotions and thrive in their neurodiversity.

Promoting Emotional Resilience and Well-being

Parenting a neurodivergent child can be both rewarding and challenging. As parents, it is crucial to prioritize the emotional resilience and well-being of your child. In this subchapter, we will explore various strategies and resources to support your neurodivergent child's emotional development.

One of the key aspects of promoting emotional resilience is creating a nurturing and supportive environment at home. This can be achieved by establishing routines, setting clear expectations, and providing consistency. Consistency helps neurodivergent children feel secure and reduces anxiety, allowing them to develop emotional resilience.

Furthermore, it is essential to provide your child with opportunities to develop social skills. Social skills training programs and activities can help neurodivergent children build meaningful relationships and improve their communication abilities. Encourage your child to participate in group activities, engage in cooperative play, and practice social interactions regularly.

Additionally, teaching emotional regulation strategies is vital for neurodivergent children. These strategies can include deep breathing exercises, sensory breaks, and mindfulness practices. By helping your child understand and manage their emotions, you are equipping them with lifelong skills that will benefit their overall well-being.

Speech and language therapy can also play a significant role in supporting your child's emotional development. Communication challenges are common among neurodivergent children, and speech therapy can assist in improving their expressive and receptive language skills. Enhanced communication abilities can reduce frustration and enhance emotional regulation.

Occupational therapy can be another valuable resource for your child. Occupational therapists can help develop sensory processing strategies, fine motor skills, and self- regulation techniques. These interventions can aid in reducing sensory overload and improving emotional well-being.

As parents, it is crucial to educate yourselves about your child's condition. Learning about neurodiversity, Autism Spectrum Disorder (ASD), Attention Deficit Hyperactivity Disorder (ADHD), and learning disabilities will help you better understand your child's needs. Seek out resources, support groups, and workshops specifically tailored for parents of neurodivergent children. Connecting with other parents who share similar experiences can provide emotional support and valuable insights.

Finally, remember to take care of your own well-being as well. Parenting a neurodivergent child can be physically and emotionally demanding. Ensure that you have a support system in place and take time for self-care activities. By prioritizing your well-being, you will be better equipped to support your child effectively.

Promoting emotional resilience and well-being is a lifelong journey. By implementing these strategies and utilizing available resources, you are providing your neurodivergent child with the tools they need to thrive emotionally and lead fulfilling lives.

Chapter 9: Speech and Language Therapy for Neurodivergent Children

Understanding Speech and Language Disorders

Speech and language disorders are common challenges faced by neurodivergent children. These disorders can significantly impact their ability to communicate effectively, express themselves, and engage with others. As parents of neurodivergent children, it is essential to have a deep understanding of these disorders and the various interventions available to support their development.

One of the most well-known neurodivergent conditions that often co-occurs with speech and language disorders is Autism Spectrum Disorder (ASD). Children with ASD may experience difficulties with both verbal and non-verbal communication, such as delayed speech, repetitive language patterns, and challenges with understanding social cues. It is crucial for parents to seek out ASD-specific resources and support to address the unique needs of their child.

Another common condition is Attention Deficit Hyperactivity Disorder (ADHD), which can also affect speech and language development. Children with ADHD may struggle with impulsivity and maintaining attention during conversations, leading to poor communication skills. Parents can find resources and strategies specifically designed to support neurodivergent children with ADHD and their speech and language needs.

Sensory processing disorder is another challenge that can impact speech and language development. Children with sensory processing issues may struggle with processing and integrating auditory information, making it difficult for them to understand and produce speech. Interventions such as sensory-based therapies can help address these challenges and improve communication skills.

Learning disabilities can also have a profound impact on speech and language development. These disabilities may affect a child's ability to process and understand language, resulting in difficulties with reading, writing, and verbal expression. Parents can explore various interventions and educational support to help their child overcome these challenges and develop their language skills.

Executive functioning skills and social skills training are vital for neurodivergent children to improve their communication abilities. These interventions focus on teaching skills such as turn-taking, active listening, and understanding non-verbal cues. Additionally, emotional regulation strategies can assist children in expressing themselves more effectively and managing their emotions during communication.

Speech and language therapy and occupational therapy are essential interventions for neurodivergent children with speech and language disorders. These therapies aim to improve communication skills, enhance articulation, and develop language abilities through targeted exercises and interventions.

Lastly, parents play a crucial role in supporting their neurodivergent children's speech and language development. By utilizing effective parenting strategies, such as providing a supportive and nurturing environment, actively listening to their child, and using visual aids and communication tools, parents can facilitate their child's communication and language growth.

Understanding speech and language disorders is essential for parents of neurodivergent children. By seeking out appropriate resources and interventions, parents can support their child's communication journey and help them reach their full potential.

Early Intervention and Assessment

In the journey of raising neurodivergent children, early intervention and assessment play a vital role in providing the necessary support and resources for their development.
Understanding the unique needs of your child and identifying their strengths and challenges at an early age is crucial for designing effective interventions and creating a nurturing environment.

Assessment is the first step in this process. It involves a comprehensive evaluation by professionals who specialize in neurodiversity, such as psychologists, pediatricians, and therapists. Through various assessments, they can determine the presence of conditions such as Autism Spectrum Disorder (ASD), Attention Deficit Hyperactivity Disorder (ADHD), sensory processing disorder, learning disabilities, and more. This assessment helps provide a clearer picture of your child's strengths and areas that require support.

Once the assessment is completed, early intervention becomes the next focus. Early intervention refers to the range of services and interventions designed to support the development of neurodivergent children from birth to their school years. It encompasses a multidisciplinary approach that addresses different aspects of a child's development, including cognitive, communication, social, emotional, and motor skills.

For children with ASD, early intervention might involve specialized therapies, such as Applied Behavior Analysis (ABA), which focuses on enhancing communication and social skills. In the case of ADHD, interventions may include behavioral strategies, such as creating routines and providing organizational tools. Similarly, sensory processing disorder interventions aim to help children manage sensory stimuli and regulate their responses effectively.

Learning disabilities assistance involves tailored strategies to accommodate individual learning styles and provide additional support in academic settings. Executive functioning skills development targets skills like organization, time management, and planning. Social skills training helps children navigate social interactions and develop meaningful relationships. Emotional regulation strategies focus on teaching children how to identify and manage their emotions effectively.

Speech and language therapy is often a critical component of early intervention, as it supports communication development in neurodivergent children. Occupational therapy helps children develop fine motor skills, sensory integration, and self-help skills, enabling them to participate more fully in daily activities.

While professionals play a crucial role in early intervention and assessment, parents also have a significant impact on their child's progress. Parenting strategies that promote understanding, acceptance, and empathy are essential. Creating a supportive and inclusive environment at home, establishing routines, and providing a safe space for communication and expression can make a significant difference in a child's development.

In conclusion, early intervention and assessment are pivotal in supporting the growth and development of neurodivergent children. By identifying their unique strengths and challenges early on, parents can access appropriate resources and interventions to help their child thrive. Together with professionals, parents can create a nurturing environment that fosters their child's abilities and empowers them to reach their full potential.

Speech Therapy Techniques and Exercises

Speech therapy is a vital intervention for neurodivergent children, including those with Autism Spectrum Disorder (ASD), Attention Deficit Hyperactivity Disorder (ADHD), sensory processing disorders, learning disabilities, and other developmental challenges. This subchapter will explore various speech therapy techniques and exercises that can help improve communication skills in neurodivergent children.

1. Articulation Exercises: These exercises focus on improving the clarity of speech by targeting specific sounds or phonemes. Speech therapists use various techniques such as tongue twisters, oral motor exercises, and repetitive sound production to help children articulate words more accurately.

2. Verbal and Nonverbal Communication Strategies: Speech therapists work on enhancing both verbal and nonverbal communication skills. They teach children how to use eye contact, gestures, facial expressions, and body language to effectively express themselves and understand others.

3. Social Skills Training: Communication and social skills often go hand in hand. Speech therapists incorporate social skills training into their sessions, helping children develop skills like turn-taking, active listening, initiating and maintaining conversations, and understanding social cues.

4. Augmentative and Alternative Communication (AAC) Tools: For children who struggle with verbal communication, AAC tools can be incredibly beneficial. These tools include sign language, picture exchange systems, communication boards, and speech-generating devices. Speech therapists can help children and parents learn how to use these tools effectively.

5. Language Expansion and Development: Speech therapists help children expand their language skills by introducing new vocabulary, teaching grammar rules, and promoting sentence structure. They use various activities like storytelling, role-playing, and picture-based exercises to enhance language development.

6. Pronunciation and Intonation Practice: Some neurodivergent children may struggle with proper pronunciation and intonation. Speech therapists utilize techniques like modeling, repetition, and auditory feedback to improve these skills, ensuring that children are understood by others and can express themselves with clarity.

7. Parent Involvement: Speech therapy is most effective when parents actively participate in their child's sessions and continue practicing techniques at home. Speech therapists provide parents with resources, exercises, and strategies to reinforce therapy goals and facilitate progress outside of therapy sessions.

Remember, every child is unique, and speech therapy techniques should be tailored to their specific needs and goals. Working closely with a qualified speech therapist can help parents navigate the challenges and ensure that their neurodivergent child receives the support they need to thrive in their communication skills.

Supporting Language Development and Communication Skills

Navigating Neurodiversity: A Guide for Parents of Neurodivergent Children

Language development and communication skills play a crucial role in the overall development of neurodivergent children. In this subchapter, we will explore various strategies and resources that can assist parents in fostering effective communication and language skills in their neurodivergent children.

For children with Autism Spectrum Disorder (ASD), language development can often be a challenge. However, there are numerous supports available to help them overcome these difficulties. Speech and language therapy can be highly beneficial, as it focuses on enhancing communication skills, improving social interactions, and building vocabulary. Additionally, social skills training can aid in teaching essential communication and interaction skills necessary for daily life.

Children with Attention Deficit Hyperactivity Disorder (ADHD) may struggle with expressing themselves and understanding others. To support their language development, parents can implement strategies such as breaking down instructions into smaller, manageable tasks, using visual aids, and providing consistent and clear communication. These techniques can help improve their understanding and facilitate effective communication.

Sensory processing disorder interventions can also contribute to language development. Occupational therapy can assist in addressing sensory challenges, which in turn may positively impact language skills. By creating a sensory-friendly environment and incorporating sensory activities into daily routines, parents can create opportunities for their children to engage in meaningful communication.

Learning disabilities can present obstacles to language development, but with the right assistance, progress can be made. Parents can seek out resources that focus on specific learning disabilities and tailor interventions accordingly. By providing individualized support and using multisensory teaching methods, parents can help their children develop and strengthen language skills.

Executive functioning skills are vital for effective communication and language development. Parents can assist their children in developing these skills by breaking tasks into smaller steps, setting goals, and providing visual schedules. Additionally, practicing emotional regulation strategies and implementing routines can also aid in language development and communication.

Throughout this subchapter, we will also explore the role of speech and language therapy and how it can benefit neurodivergent children. We will discuss the importance of occupational therapy in supporting language development and explore various parenting strategies that can be employed to raise neurodivergent children effectively.

By implementing these strategies and utilizing available resources, parents can play a fundamental role in supporting language development and communication skills in their neurodivergent children.

Chapter 10: Occupational Therapy for Neurodivergent Children

Understanding Occupational Therapy and its Benefits

Occupational therapy (OT) is a highly beneficial and widely recognized intervention for neurodivergent children. In this subchapter, we will explore the ins and outs of occupational therapy, its benefits, and how it can positively impact the lives of your neurodivergent child.

Occupational therapy focuses on developing and enhancing the skills necessary for daily living, such as self-care, social interaction, and academic performance. It aims to maximize your child's independence and overall well-being by addressing their unique challenges and needs.

For children with Autism Spectrum Disorder (ASD), occupational therapy can provide valuable support. It helps them develop social skills, manage sensory sensitivities, and improve communication abilities. Through various sensory integration techniques, occupational therapists can assist your child in regulating their responses to sensory stimuli, reducing anxiety and meltdowns.

Attention Deficit Hyperactivity Disorder (ADHD) often comes with difficulties in executive functioning skills, such as organization, time management, and impulse control.
Occupational therapy can help your child improve these skills and develop strategies to manage their ADHD symptoms effectively.

Sensory processing disorder (SPD) interventions are integral to occupational therapy. Occupational therapists work closely with your child to address their sensory sensitivities and help them better navigate their environment. By creating sensory diets and engaging in sensory integration activities, your child can learn to self-regulate and focus on their daily tasks.

Learning disabilities can significantly impact a child's academic performance. Occupational therapy offers specialized interventions to support their cognitive and academic development. Therapists use various techniques, such as adaptive equipment and assistive technology, to enhance your child's learning experience and academic success.

Executive functioning skills, including planning, organization, and problem-solving, are essential for neurodivergent children. Occupational therapy can assist in the development of these skills, allowing your child to become more independent and self- reliant.

Social skills training is another crucial aspect of occupational therapy. Therapists use role- playing, group activities, and social stories to teach your child appropriate social behaviors, communication skills, and emotional regulation strategies.

Occupational therapy also encompasses speech and language therapy. Therapists work on improving your child's communication abilities, including speech production, language comprehension, and social pragmatic skills.

As parents of neurodivergent children, it is crucial to understand the benefits of occupational therapy. It offers a holistic approach to addressing your child's unique needs, fostering their development, and enhancing their overall quality of life. By incorporating occupational therapy into your child's treatment plan, you can provide them with the necessary tools to thrive and succeed.

Assessing Sensory Integration and Motor Skills

Understanding the sensory integration and motor skills of neurodivergent children is crucial for their overall development and well-being. In this subchapter, we will explore the importance of assessing these skills and provide insights into various interventions and strategies that can support your neurodivergent child.

Sensory integration refers to the brain's ability to process and organize information received through the senses. Neurodivergent children, such as those with Autism Spectrum Disorder (ASD), often experience challenges in sensory processing, which can affect their daily functioning. By assessing their sensory integration abilities, parents can gain valuable insights into their child's sensitivities, preferences, and areas of difficulty.

Motor skills, on the other hand, involve the coordination of muscles and movements. Neurodivergent children may struggle with fine motor skills, such as writing or buttoning clothes, or gross motor skills, like balancing or jumping. Assessing motor skills can help identify specific areas of difficulty and guide interventions to improve their physical abilities.

There are various assessment tools and professionals available to help evaluate sensory integration and motor skills. Occupational therapists specialize in supporting neurodivergent children and can conduct comprehensive assessments to determine their sensory processing abilities and motor skills. These assessments may include observations, standardized tests, and parent or teacher questionnaires.

Once the assessment is completed, parents can work with professionals to develop individualized interventions and strategies. For sensory processing difficulties, interventions may include sensory diets, which involve providing specific sensory experiences to help regulate the child's sensory system. Occupational therapy can also address motor skill challenges through activities that promote coordination, strength, and balance.

In addition to professional support, parents can implement strategies at home to support their child's sensory integration and motor skills. Creating a sensory-friendly environment with appropriate lighting, sound, and textures can help regulate sensory input. Encouraging play and physical activities that target specific motor skills can also contribute to their development.

It is important to remember that every child is unique, and what works for one may not work for another. Regular reassessment and adapting interventions as needed is crucial. Patience, understanding, and a supportive environment are key to helping your neurodivergent child thrive.

In conclusion, assessing sensory integration and motor skills is essential for understanding your neurodivergent child's unique needs and supporting their development. Collaborating with professionals, implementing strategies at home, and providing a nurturing environment can contribute to their overall well-being and success. Remember, you are not alone in this journey, and there are resources and support available to help you navigate the challenges and celebrate the strengths of your neurodivergent child.

Occupational Therapy Interventions and Activities

Navigating Neurodiversity: A Guide for Parents of Neurodivergent Children

Occupational therapy (OT) is a valuable and effective intervention for neurodivergent children, including those with Autism Spectrum Disorder (ASD), Attention Deficit Hyperactivity Disorder (ADHD), sensory processing disorder, learning disabilities, and more. It focuses on helping children develop the skills they need to participate in everyday activities at home, school, and in their community.

One of the main goals of occupational therapy is to enhance a child's ability to function independently and improve their overall quality of life. Occupational therapists work closely with parents to create individualized treatment plans that address specific needs and goals for each child.

Sensory integration therapy is an important component of occupational therapy for neurodivergent children. This therapy helps children who struggle with sensory processing difficulties by providing them with activities and exercises that help regulate and organize their sensory experiences. This may include activities such as swinging, jumping, and playing with different textures to help them become more comfortable and better able to engage with their environment.

In addition to sensory integration therapy, occupational therapists also focus on developing executive functioning skills in neurodivergent children. These skills include attention, organization, planning, and problem-solving abilities. By using various strategies and activities, occupational therapists can help children develop these skills, which are crucial for academic success and daily life tasks.

Social skills training is another important aspect of occupational therapy. Many neurodivergent children struggle with social interactions, and occupational therapists can provide them with the necessary tools and strategies to improve their social skills. This may involve role-playing, social stories, and group activities to help children practice and develop appropriate social behaviors.

Occupational therapy also addresses emotional regulation strategies for neurodivergent children. Many children with neurodivergent conditions struggle with managing their emotions, and occupational therapists can teach them coping mechanisms and techniques to regulate their emotions in a healthy and constructive way.

Speech and language therapy is often integrated into occupational therapy for neurodivergent children who have communication difficulties. Occupational therapists work alongside speech-language pathologists to help children improve their speech and language skills, facilitating better communication and social interactions.

Overall, occupational therapy is a multifaceted approach that addresses various aspects of a neurodivergent child's development. By incorporating sensory integration therapy, executive functioning skills development, social skills training, emotional regulation strategies, and speech and language therapy, occupational therapists provide comprehensive support to help children thrive and reach their full potential.

As parents, it is important to collaborate with occupational therapists and actively participate in the therapy process. This may include implementing strategies and activities learned during therapy sessions at home, advocating for your child's needs, and seeking additional resources and support as necessary.

By utilizing the interventions and activities provided by occupational therapy, parents can play a crucial role in supporting the growth and development of their neurodivergent children. With the right strategies and support, these children can overcome challenges, build essential skills, and lead fulfilling lives.

Supporting Daily Living Skills and Independence

In this subchapter, we will discuss various strategies and resources to support the daily living skills and independence of neurodivergent children. Whether your child has Autism Spectrum Disorder (ASD), Attention Deficit Hyperactivity Disorder (ADHD), sensory processing disorder, learning disabilities, or any other neurodivergent condition, these tips and interventions can help promote their overall development.

1. Establish routines: Creating structured daily routines can provide a sense of predictability and stability for your child. Break down tasks into manageable steps and use visual schedules or timers to help them understand and follow the routine.

2. Develop executive functioning skills: Executive functioning skills are crucial for planning, organizing, and managing daily tasks. Encourage your child to break down tasks into smaller parts, use checklists, and practice time management techniques. Teach them strategies to prioritize tasks and set goals.

3. Provide sensory supports: Sensory processing difficulties can significantly impact a child's daily life. Consult with an occupational therapist to identify sensory triggers and develop appropriate interventions. This may include providing sensory breaks, using sensory-friendly materials, or implementing sensory diets.

4. Foster independence: Encourage your child to take on age-appropriate responsibilities. Start by teaching them basic self-care skills like dressing, grooming, and feeding themselves. Gradually introduce new tasks and provide ample support and praise for their efforts.

5. Enhance social skills: Neurodivergent children may struggle with social interactions. Consider enrolling them in social skills training programs or groups tailored to their specific needs. Provide opportunities for structured playdates and coach them on appropriate social behaviors.

6. Support emotional regulation: Help your child develop strategies to manage their emotions effectively. This may involve teaching deep breathing exercises, providing a calm-down corner, or introducing mindfulness techniques. Encourage open communication and validate their feelings.

7. Access therapy services: Speech and language therapy and occupational therapy can be invaluable for neurodivergent children. These therapies can help improve communication, fine motor skills, and sensory integration. Consult with professionals to determine the most suitable therapy options for your child.

8. Employ parenting strategies: Parenting a neurodivergent child can be challenging, and it is essential to equip yourself with effective strategies. Educate yourself about your child's specific condition, seek support from other parents or support groups, and practice self-care to maintain your own well-being.

Remember, every child is unique, and what works for one may not work for another. Experiment with different strategies, be patient, and celebrate your child's progress, no matter how small. With the right support and resources, your child can develop daily living skills and gain independence, empowering them to thrive in their own unique way.

Chapter 11: Parenting Strategies for Raising Neurodivergent Children

Embracing a Strengths-Based Approach

In navigating the journey of raising a neurodivergent child, it is essential for parents to embrace a strengths-based approach. This approach focuses on recognizing and nurturing the unique strengths and abilities that neurodivergent children possess, rather than solely focusing on their challenges. By shifting the perspective towards strengths, parents can unlock their child's full potential and promote their overall well-being.

Autism Spectrum Disorder (ASD) support for neurodivergent children:
For parents of children with ASD, embracing a strengths-based approach means understanding and appreciating the unique abilities and interests that often accompany this condition. By identifying their child's strengths, such as exceptional attention to detail or a special talent in a specific area, parents can provide opportunities for growth and success.

Attention Deficit Hyperactivity Disorder (ADHD) resources for neurodivergent children: When it comes to ADHD, a strengths-based approach entails recognizing the positive attributes associated with this condition, such as high energy levels and creativity. By channeling these strengths into productive activities and providing structure and support, parents can help their ADHD child thrive.

Navigating Neurodiversity: A Guide for Parents of Neurodivergent Children

Sensory processing disorder interventions for neurodivergent children:
For children with sensory processing disorders, a strengths-based approach involves creating an environment that acknowledges and accommodates their unique sensory needs. By identifying activities or environments that provide comfort and sensory regulation, parents can empower their child to navigate the world with confidence.

Learning disabilities assistance for neurodivergent children:
With learning disabilities, a strengths-based approach involves identifying and nurturing the areas where the child excels. By focusing on their strengths, parents can build their child's confidence and self-esteem, enabling them to overcome challenges and achieve academic success.

Executive functioning skills development for neurodivergent children:
When it comes to developing executive functioning skills in neurodivergent children, a strengths-based approach involves recognizing and building upon their inherent strengths, such as problem-solving abilities or creativity. By providing appropriate support and strategies, parents can help their child develop essential executive functioning skills, such as planning, organization, and time management.

Social skills training for neurodivergent children:
In social skills training, a strengths-based approach involves identifying and nurturing the social strengths of neurodivergent children, such as empathy or a unique perspective. By focusing on these strengths, parents can help their child develop meaningful connections and navigate social interactions successfully.

Emotional regulation strategies for neurodivergent children:
When supporting neurodivergent children in managing their emotions, a strengths-based approach involves recognizing and building upon their emotional strengths, such as empathy or resilience. By providing tools and strategies that align with their strengths, parents can empower their child to regulate their emotions effectively.

Speech and language therapy for neurodivergent children:
In speech and language therapy, a strengths-based approach involves utilizing the child's existing communication strengths to facilitate growth. By focusing on their strengths, such as non-verbal communication or visual learning, parents can support their child's language development effectively.

Occupational therapy for neurodivergent children:
In occupational therapy, a strengths-based approach involves identifying and building upon the child's strengths and interests to improve their daily functioning and independence. By incorporating activities that align with their strengths, parents can help their child develop essential life skills.

Parenting strategies for raising neurodivergent children:
Overall, embracing a strengths-based approach in parenting neurodivergent children means recognizing and valuing their unique strengths rather than focusing solely on their challenges. By emphasizing their strengths, parents can provide the support and guidance necessary for their child's growth and success.

Building a Supportive Network of Professionals and Peers

Navigating Neurodiversity: A Guide for Parents of Neurodivergent Children

As parents of neurodivergent children, we understand the unique challenges and joys that come with raising our exceptional kids. Navigating Neurodiversity is here to provide guidance and support as you navigate the journey of parenting a neurodivergent child. In this subchapter, we will discuss the importance of building a supportive network of professionals and peers.

One of the most valuable resources for parents is connecting with professionals who specialize in working with neurodivergent children. Whether it's a pediatrician, therapist, or educational specialist, these professionals can offer invaluable insights and guidance tailored to your child's specific needs. They can help you understand your child's diagnosis, offer strategies for managing challenging behaviors, and provide recommendations for appropriate interventions and therapies.

Autism Spectrum Disorder (ASD) support for neurodivergent children is a crucial aspect of building a supportive network. Seek out professionals who are experienced in working with children on the spectrum, such as behavioral therapists, speech and language pathologists, and occupational therapists. These professionals can provide interventions and strategies that focus on improving communication skills, social interactions, and sensory processing.

For children with Attention Deficit Hyperactivity Disorder (ADHD), it is important to connect with professionals who specialize in ADHD resources. These professionals can provide strategies for managing impulsivity, improving attention and focus, and implementing effective behavior management techniques.

Additionally, parents of neurodivergent children may benefit from connecting with other parents who are on a similar journey. Peer support groups or online communities can provide a safe space to share experiences, exchange advice, and offer emotional support. It is incredibly empowering to connect with other parents who have faced similar challenges and triumphs, as they can offer a unique understanding and perspective.

Remember, you are not alone in this journey. By building a supportive network of professionals and peers, you are equipping yourself with the tools and resources necessary to navigate the ups and downs of raising a neurodivergent child. Embrace the power of community and seek out those who can provide the guidance and support you need. Together, we can create a world that celebrates neurodiversity and supports our exceptional children.

In the next subchapter, we will explore various interventions and strategies that can aid in the development of executive functioning skills in neurodivergent children. Stay tuned for more valuable insights and practical tips in Navigating Neurodiversity: A Guide for Parents of Neurodivergent Children.

Practicing Self-Care and Stress Management

Introduction:
As parents of neurodivergent children, it is important to prioritize your own well-being in order to better support and care for your child. Navigating the challenges of raising neurodivergent children can be overwhelming and stressful at times. This subchapter will focus on the importance of practicing self-care and stress management techniques specifically tailored to parents of neurodivergent children. By taking care of yourself, you will be better equipped to provide the necessary support and resources for your child's unique needs.

Navigating Neurodiversity: A Guide for Parents of Neurodivergent Children

Self-Care:

Self-care is not a luxury, but a necessity for parents of neurodivergent children. It involves making time for yourself, engaging in activities that bring you joy and relaxation, and maintaining a healthy work-life balance. By prioritizing self-care, you are not being selfish, but rather ensuring that you have the energy and emotional resilience to meet the demands of parenting.

Stress Management Techniques:

1. Seek Support: Connect with other parents who are also raising neurodivergent children. Support groups and online communities can provide a safe space to share experiences, seek advice, and offer support to one another.

2. Practice Mindfulness: Incorporate mindfulness techniques into your daily routine. This can include deep breathing exercises, meditation, or simply taking a moment to focus on the present and let go of worries or stressors.

3. Take Breaks: It is important to take breaks when needed to recharge and reduce stress. Create a schedule that allows for regular breaks throughout the day, whether it's going for a walk, reading a book, or pursuing a hobby.

4. Establish Boundaries: Set clear boundaries with yourself and others to prevent burnout. Learn to say no when necessary and prioritize your own needs without feeling guilty.

5. Engage in Physical Activity: Regular exercise has been proven to reduce stress and improve overall well-being. Find an activity that you enjoy, whether it's yoga, running, or dancing, and make it a part of your routine.

Conclusion:

Practicing self-care and stress management is crucial for parents of neurodivergent children. By prioritizing your own well-being, you are better equipped to support your child's unique needs. Remember, self-care is not selfish but necessary for your own mental, emotional, and physical health. Implement these strategies into your daily life and watch as your ability to navigate the challenges of raising a neurodivergent child improves.

Advocating for Your Child's Needs

As parents of neurodivergent children, one of the most important roles you have is to be an advocate for your child's needs. Navigating Neurodiversity: A Guide for Parents of Neurodivergent Children is here to provide you with the tools and resources to effectively advocate for your child, whether they have Autism Spectrum Disorder (ASD), Attention Deficit Hyperactivity Disorder (ADHD), sensory processing disorder, learning disabilities, or any other neurodivergent condition.

Advocacy begins with understanding your child's unique needs and strengths. Educate yourself about their diagnosis, learn about the challenges they may face, and stay updated on the latest research and interventions available. By arming yourself with knowledge, you can confidently advocate for your child's rights within various settings, including schools, healthcare providers, and community organizations.

Navigating Neurodiversity: A Guide for Parents of Neurodivergent Children

One essential aspect of advocacy is ensuring your child receives appropriate support and resources. For children on the autism spectrum, this may involve seeking out ASD-specific support services that cater to their unique needs. Likewise, ADHD resources can provide strategies for managing attention and hyperactivity challenges. Sensory processing disorder interventions can help your child navigate sensory sensitivities that may cause distress. Learning disabilities assistance can provide accommodations and strategies to help your child succeed academically.

Executive functioning skills are crucial for neurodivergent children, and by working with professionals, you can develop strategies to enhance their planning, organization, and time management abilities. Social skills training is also important, as it can help your child navigate social interactions and build meaningful relationships. Emotional regulation strategies are invaluable tools for neurodivergent children, teaching them how to manage and express their emotions effectively.

Therapies such as speech and language therapy and occupational therapy can greatly benefit neurodivergent children, addressing communication challenges and enhancing motor skills, respectively. These therapies can be instrumental in helping your child reach their full potential.

Lastly, this subchapter will explore parenting strategies specifically tailored to raising neurodivergent children. It will provide insights on fostering a supportive and inclusive environment at home, effectively managing challenging behaviors, and promoting self-esteem and independence.

Remember, advocating for your child's needs is a continuous process. By staying informed, collaborating with professionals, and being their voice, you can ensure your child receives the support they require to thrive in a neurodiverse world.

Nurturing Resilience and Confidence in Neurodivergent Children

When it comes to raising neurodivergent children, one of the most important goals for parents is to help them develop resilience and confidence. Neurodivergent children, such as those with Autism Spectrum Disorder (ASD), Attention Deficit Hyperactivity Disorder (ADHD), sensory processing disorder, learning disabilities, or executive functioning challenges, often face unique struggles in their daily lives. However, with the right support and strategies, parents can empower their children to thrive and build a strong sense of self.

Resilience is the ability to bounce back from challenges and adapt to new situations. It is a crucial skill for neurodivergent children, as they may encounter difficulties in various aspects of their lives. One way parents can nurture resilience is by fostering a supportive and inclusive environment at home. This involves creating predictable routines, providing clear expectations, and offering praise and encouragement for small achievements. By celebrating their child's successes, parents can help them develop a positive mindset and the belief that they can overcome obstacles.

Confidence is another key aspect of a neurodivergent child's development. Building confidence begins with recognizing and celebrating their unique strengths and abilities. Parents can help their child discover their passions and interests, and provide opportunities for them to pursue those activities. By engaging in activities that align with their strengths, neurodivergent children can experience success, which in turn boosts their self-esteem and confidence.

Navigating Neurodiversity: A Guide for Parents of Neurodivergent Children

In addition to creating a supportive environment, parents can also utilize various resources and interventions to further enhance their child's resilience and confidence. Speech and language therapy can help improve communication skills, while occupational therapy can address sensory processing difficulties. Learning disabilities assistance can provide strategies to overcome academic challenges, and executive functioning skills development can help with organization and time management. Social skills training can support neurodivergent children in building meaningful relationships, and emotional regulation strategies can teach them how to manage their emotions effectively.

It is equally important for parents to equip themselves with effective parenting strategies when raising neurodivergent children. This includes practicing self-care, seeking support from professionals and support groups, and staying informed about the latest research and therapies. By taking care of their own well-being, parents can better support their child's needs and model resilience and confidence.

In conclusion, nurturing resilience and confidence in neurodivergent children is a crucial aspect of their overall development. By creating a supportive environment, utilizing resources and interventions, and implementing effective parenting strategies, parents can empower their child to navigate life's challenges with resilience and confidence.
With the right guidance and support, neurodivergent children can thrive and reach their full potential.